COACHING ARCHERY

FOR BEGINNING TO INTERMEDIATE COACHES

Coaching Archery

COACHING ARCHERY

FOR BEGINNING TO INTERMEDIATE COACHES

by **Steve Ruis**

Editor of Archery Focus Magazine

WATCHING ARROWS FLY, LLC

Library of Congress Cataloging-in Publication Data

Coaching Archery / Steve Ruis.
p. cm
Includes bibliographic references and index.
ISBN 978-0-9821471-0-8 (softcover)
1. Archery. 2. Coaching. I Steve Ruis, 1946-

ISBN: 978-0-9821471-0-8

The web addresses cited in this text were current as of August 2008, unless otherwise noted.

Writer: Steve Ruis; **Copy Editor**; Steve Ruis; **Proofreader**: Claudia Stevenson; **Graphic Artist**: Steve Ruis; **Cover Designer**: Steve Ruis; **Photographers** (cover and interior): Steve Ruis and Claudia Stevenson unless otherwise noted; **Illustrator** Steve Ruis

Printed in the United States of America 10 9 8 7 6 5 4 3 2 1

Watching Arrows Fly
3712 North Broadway, #285
Chicago, IL 60613
800.671.1140

WATCHING ARROWS FLY, LLC

Dedication

It is a rare gift to be able to live with your inspiration. Claudia Stevenson and I have been partners in business and life for almost 20 years. We share everything to the extent that you will read me referring to myself as "I" in places and "We" in other places. This is not the royal "We'" and I am not putting on airs; it is just that Claudia and I have discussed so many of these matters and come to common understandings that "I" and "We" are frequently interchangeable.

This book is dedicated to her.

(But don't blame her for anything I put in this book; some things I do by myself.)

Steve Ruis
June 2008

Contents

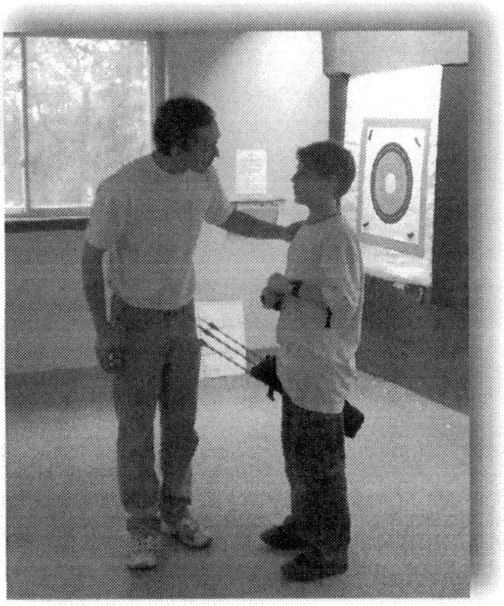

Introduction

Why "Coaching Archery"?

I recently did an Amazon.com search for books on "coaching." That search had 21,363 hits. Apparently coaching is a popular topic on which to write. I then searched for "coaching archery." This is what I got:

Teaching Archery (by Haywood and Lewis) A book long out of print.

Archery (by Jean Barrett) An archery book, but ... not a coaching book.

Professional Archery Technique (by Kirk Etheridge) An excellent archery book but also ... not a coaching book.

Lonely Planet Canada Huh?

The Six Wives of Henry VIII Gosh, Henry the Eighth was a big supporter of archery ... but ... gee whiz!

In other words, there *aren't* any books for beginning-to-intermediate archery coaches. There is a great deal of material for elite athletes and coaches, but little on archery there, too. So I decided to write such a book; it is needed.

What Can You Expect from This Book?

The few archery coaching books I have been able to find often try to teach you *what* you need to know. I am not going to do this, because I don't think a book is the right way to learn what you need to know to coach people. And, this book would have to be much, much bigger than it is. I am going to try to tell you what you need, not to *know*, but to *learn*. I hope to encourage, inspire, cajole, and show you how to go out and get the knowledge, skills, and attitudes you need to be a very good archery coach.

Plus, there is a huge amount of material written about the "what" of archery: what a coach needs to know, what an archer needs to know, and almost nothing on *how* to teach it. But don't get nervous, if you are reading this, this book is for you. I know this because not too many people will walk through a bookstore, see a book entitled "Coaching Archery," and pick it up thinking "Gee, I wonder what that is all about?" I imagine that you have some experience as an archery coach and/or some training already under your belt . . . or not. This book is for beginning to intermediate archery coaches. If your fantasy is to coach at the Olympics or the World Championships, well, coaching at the elite level is a whole different ball game. (If this is your fantasy, look into the trainings USA Archery and/or FITA, the International Archery Federation, provide.) This book is for people wanting to improve their coaching skills to help beginning to intermediate archers of all ages, which is a stage all aspiring elite coaches go through.

Oh, and there are more than a few repetitions in this book as I don't expect you to sit down and read it cover to cover. That would be nice, but if you were to jump to any one of the chapters you find intriguing, I didn't want you to find me referring you all over the place to get key points you missed. (I have always found that irritating and assumed you do, too.)

Why Coach?

Every summer well over 7000 new archery coaches are trained in the U.S. You would think we'd be up to our hips in archery coaches! On the contrary, there is a great need for quality coaching that remains unfulfilled. Most of those 7000+ new coaches are college students preparing for jobs at summer camps which have archery programs. Most don't continue coaching past those camp counselor jobs. (Pay attention, now; here is where you come in.) Every summer 1.8 million kids get exposed to archery in summer camps. Up to now there weren't places for them to continue in the sport, but the After School Archery Program (ASAP) is creating thousands of archery programs in park and recreation centers. There is, at the same time, a rapidly expanding demand for coaching in the form of the National Archery in Schools Program (NASP). This program, started by the Fish and Wildlife Department of the state of Kentucky has gone national (even international). Many thousands of school children are receiving their first instruction in our sport and they are loving it. The problem is there aren't enough programs available to these kids when the school program, usually just a few weeks in duration, ends. But this is what ASAP is for so, if you like kids, there will be work for you!

If you would rather work with adults, I feel there is a huge market, currently unfulfilled, for adult target archery. In my opinion, archery is the sport for the new millennium. Americans work more hours than the citizens of any other industrialized society. Their jobs have more mental stress and are more demanding than ever before. Imagine yourself to be one of these workers. (I know, it's a stretch, but try.) If, when you came home (or on the way home), you stopped and shot arrows for 15-20 minutes, you would find all of the stresses of the day gone. The focus required to execute good shots causes all of those other things to recede into the background. Later, those things would reenter your mind roughly in their order of importance to you. It is amazing. Archery is the sport for stressed out professionals, office workers, contractors, secretaries, bankers, at-home moms and dads, you name it.

We have gotten many parents into archery because their children seemed to be having so much fun. Those parents also see how their children benefit from a sport that emphasizes safety, responsibility, and discipline. Archery is the ultimate self-improvement activity! If you are standing in a book store reading this, look over at the self-improvement section. It is the largest segment of most bookstores' business. Shooting a bow is reflective. Everything you (and only you) do affects the shot. You can't blame anyone else or, for that matter, even blame yourself. You must accept the last shot and go on to the next. The bow teaches you what to do, if you can be quiet and listen to it.

If you were to start up an evening program for adults, you will not want for students if you have any kind of population base around you. And since these are customers who are used to paying for services, you will make money (if you want to).

The archery equipment market is so heavily directed at bowhunters, that there are virtually no efforts being made to bring recreational archers into the sport. A program set up through your local recreation department or archery pro shop will draw people from miles around. It is a wide open field.

Why Should *I* Coach?

This seems like a strange kind of question, seeing as how you are reading this book (and possibly already coaching archery), but it is a very important question. You must ask it, and a whole lot of other questions, before you commit to coaching as a vocation or avocation because if you don't, such questions will rise up and bite you later. Here is a sampling of the questions you need to address:

- What is coaching?
- What are my coaching fantasies?
- Is it for me?
- Who the heck am I to think I can coach? Shouldn't I be a champion first? (People will say this to your face! Rude people!)

Here's an informal check list to help you with your decision to go deeper into coaching:

- ❑ Do you like people?
- ❑ Do you like kids?
- ❑ Do you like archery?
- ❑ Do you like standing out in the hot sun?
- ❑ Do you like traveling?
- ❑ Do you like helping people?
- ❑ Do you like getting paid for doing what you love?
- ❑ Do you find archery equipment interesting?
- ❑ Do you like adapting activities for disabled students?

If you checked any of the above boxes, your mother didn't teach you, as mine did, to never write in books! Actually, no one of the above is a deal breaker. All coaches have strengths and weaknesses. You don't have to be good at, or even like, some of the aspects of coaching archery. You can be part of a team in which you work with more advanced archers and others work the newbies, or vice-versa. Coaching archery is not a solitary activity, at least not the way I do it!

Oh, one more thing—if at the end of any particular chapter you seem overloaded or you don't know what to do with the information presented or you just don't know what to do to get started, I have included a section entitled "What Can I Do?" These are things to do, to read, or to view that can take you farther, fill in what's missing, or just get the ball rolling, as it were.

So, if you are ready, so am I.

Let's get started!

What Can I Do?

Things to Do

- Take a quiet moment and think about the questions raised above (What is coaching? What are my coaching fantasies? Is it for me? Who the heck am I to think I can coach? Shouldn't I be a champion first?) and come up with your answers. If you are of the inclination, write your answers in a diary or journal.
- Before you go any further, write down your coaching philosophy (why you do what you do the way you do it). It may change as you read this book and you might just find the changes interesting.

Things to Read/View

We haven't really gotten very far, but there are some general coaching resources you might be interested in. There are more in the back of the book. (🕮 means "book" and 📹 means "video")

- 🕮 *Coach's Little Book of Wisdom* by Ron Quinn
  This very little book is very big on coaching kids—highly recommended if you intend to work with younger students of archery!
- 🕮 *Coaching Kids for Dummies* by Rick Wolfe
  This book, like all general youth coaching resources is focused on team sports and, like all of the other "... For Dummies" series, is very worthwhile.

1

Getting Certified / Staying Connected

Introduction

When Claudia and I first got involved in coaching archery it was through a 4-H shooting sports program. This program involved rifle, pistol, and shotgun shooting as well as archery for 4-H kids in our somewhat rural area. The member of our club in charge of this activity asked for volunteers to help with archery. We thought, "What the heck, it is only one weekend day a month and only during the school year." So, we volunteered. In those days, 4-H didn't required "helpers" to be certified or trained, which was a good thing at the time as we weren't. (Now they do, which is a very good thing, we believe.)

Well, it wasn't long before "it is only one weekend day a month and only during the school year" turned into a complaint "it is only one weekend day a month and only during the school year." After sitting around the kitchen table repeating this same complaint to all of our archery friends for several months, I looked across the table at Claudia and found agreement to do something "for the kids."

I knew of a guy in Sacramento (50 miles away) who did coach trainings and emailed him for particulars. He needed at least six people to make a class, so we talked another five club members into joining us for a fun weekend of coach training! So, we got certified; we were "official" archery coaches. Indeed, we did learn a lot at this training, since *teaching* archery is a completely different subject from *doing* archery.

So, the next thing to consider was making up an ongoing archery program that operated weekly rather than monthly. I thought that within six months to a year we could get the necessary equipment together, arrange a training site, all the stuff we had been talking about. Claudia got together a small support group and launched the program three weeks later, with me sputtering, "But . . . , but . . . " and Claudia saying, "If you can't keep up, at least don't slow me down."

Somehow everything got done and our program was launched and was really quite successful (all thanks to Claudia; had it been up to me, we would still be making lists of Things to Do Before Launching Our Program).

So, the moral of the story is . . . if you build it, they will come, and . . . if you want to be a coach/instructor of archery students, you really need to get certified.

Getting Certified

Most of the major archery organizations offer some kind of archery coach/instructor training, which is a good thing because all of the major youth groups (Boy Scouts, Girl Scouts, 4-H, etc.) now require their instructors to be certified.

The two largest archery organizations, the National Field Archery Association (NFAA) and USA Archery (USAA) have a joint certification for the first two levels of certification. Here's how it works. There are four levels of certification:

Level 1 Beginning Archery Instructor
Level 2 Intermediate Archery Instructor
Level 3 Archery Coach
Level 4 Expert Archery Coach

They are considering changes in the titles of these certificates and small changes in their curricula, so don't get upset if they change things up a little.

The Level 1 certificate is primarily for summer camp instructors. Archery in summer camps is often taught in a program with one Level 2 Instructor and a cadre of Level 1 Instructors who, typically, are college students working a summer job. In these camps, a great many children are taught their first archery lesson. And the instructors end up teaching that first lesson over and over and over as kids cycle through the camps. So, you can see a great deal of depth of coaching knowledge and experience are not needed. Some camps have on-going programs, but the majority are set up with archery being a one-time event.

So, if you are not in this situation and you are going to be in an on-going program, the ability to skip over the Level 1 training has been provided—there's a catch, though, to do this you have to have been a participant in organized archery for a year or more. The reason this is allowed is that a substantial part of a Level 1 training is teaching the participants to shoot a bow and arrow, so if you already know how, you can skip up to the Level 2 training.

The Level 2 training takes a whole weekend, assumes you can shoot a bow (compound, recurve, or longbow), and has a test at the end of the training to measure what you have learned. With a Level 2 Certificate, USA Archery allows you to run a Junior Olympic Archery Development (JOAD) program, which is USAA's youth archery program.

The Level 3 and 4 trainings (so far) are week-long trainings, given only at Olympic Training Centers (OTCs—in California, Colorado, and New York) although there is some discussion of allowing these trainings to be given at other sites. These are USA Archery only. (The NFAA has Master Coach trainings, currently under revision, that are the rough equivalent of these trainings.) A distinction is made here between an "instructor" and a "coach." Coaches are certified to work with individuals, while instructors are certified to work with groups. Of course, instructors working with participants in their groups are working with individuals from time to time, but I think you get the idea.

The trainings at the OTCs are really cool. They cost a few hundred dollars but that includes room and board at the OTC, along with the instruction. The charge for training and your airfare and a week away from home and work are the total cost.

So, is a Level 1 Certificate with its One-day Training Good Enough?

If you are helping someone else in their program, the answer is probably yes. If you want to run your own program, you need at least a Level 2 certificate. Claudia and I created a JOAD competitive team to have some place for our more serious program archers to go (and compete). We talked one of our friends and fellow club members (a long time champion archer) into taking over the team. Since he wasn't certified, we gave him a Level 2 training. Just a few short years later, he is a Level 4 Coach and has a national reputation for being a fine youth coach. Our friend wasn't required or urged to take those trainings, he wanted to, to become a better coach. (In fact, when we first asked him to take the job, he turned us down saying, "I didn't retire to have to be somewhere any particular time of the week.") He now loves the work he is doing with some fine young people.

So, watch out, coaching archery may be addictive!

How Do I Get Started?

Getting certified is easier now than ever before because of the National Alliance for the Development of Archery (NADA). In 2001 NADA took over facilitation of Level 1 and 2 trainings for USA Archery and recently the NFAA agreed to the same arrangement. All you have to do is call NADA (352.472.2388, www.teacharchery.org) and tell them you want to get trained and they will connect you to people in your area who can do that. Keep in mind that none of us who do these trainings (Claudia and I are scheduled to do two of them in the next month as I am writing this) want to train folks one and two at a time; you might have to wait until enough people in your area want training to get one scheduled. Or you can be proactive and recruit enough people to attract a trainer.

Staying Connected

You will read here and elsewhere in this book, that to be a good archery coach, you need a support group of other coaches. These are people you have met along the way who share your interest in archery. These are also people who can help you if you get stuck on some aspect of coaching archery.

Whenever I get to talk to other coaches I get one of their cards for my files.

Every time I go to a training or seminar I collect business cards from other coaches and keep them. Occasionally I get an email from one of them or I send an email to one of them because of a problem encountered. All of these fellow coaches form a community of people who are your "support group" or your "village" as in "It takes a Village . . . to Raise a Child" (or teach him archery).

Here's my card.

There are printable business card blanks available in office supply stores, that you can print out on your computer's printer (mine is shown here). I print out about 20 at a time and when I ask a fellow coach for her card, I offer one of mine—just like in the real world! This is also a marketing tool for me as I pass them out to folks interested in paid archery lessons.

Having "helpers" at the end of a phone line or an email away is a two-way street. If you want to be able to ask questions, you should be willing to answer them, too. But this is just common sense . . . and good manners.

What Can I Do?

Things to Do

- Check out NADA's website (*www.teacharchery.org*). They are the folks who can arrange a training for you.
- On USA Archery's website (*www.usarchery.org*) where you can find a number of coaching resources including a list of their Level 3 and 4 coaches. There may be

one in your neighborhood!

Things to Read/View

If you are a subscriber to *Archery Focus* magazine, Tim Scronce (an award-winning coach of beginners) has written many articles about coaching and getting certified; here is a sample:

- Coaching . . . Why Do It? by Tim Scronce (Vol 8 No 4)
- Got Archery? by Tim Scronce (Vol 9 No 3)
- Teaching or Coaching? by Tim Scronce (Vol 10 No 3)

Your library may carry the magazine or you may ask them to carry it. The OnLine Edition comes with access to all of the back issues!

2

Safety, Safety, Safety

Introduction

You know the old joke about the New York cabbie who when asked "How do you get to Carnegie Hall?" answered "Practice, practice, practice?" Similarly, the answer to the question of "What's most important to get a good reputation as an archery coach?" is "Safety, safety, safety."

In 2005, Arrow Sport published in its newsletter *Insight* a report on several studies of sports safety. (If you would like to read the full report, you can get a full copy here: www.communityarchery.com/ArcherySafetyInsight.pdf.) In one of the studies, data from the National Electronic Injury Surveillance System (NEISS), which is under the U.S. Consumer Product Safety Commission (CPSC), was presented. NEISS is a database used to track hospital injuries for more than 15,000 kinds of consumer products used in sports and recreational activities in and around homes and schools. Of the twenty sports/activities that were noted, the three worst in injuries per 1000 participants were football (23.92), basketball (16.30), and baseball (15.98). The three best sports were table tennis (0.09), badminton (0.29), and bowling (0.31). Where was archery? Just above bowling, but below tennis (1.16) at 0.65 injuries per 1000 participants.

In another such study Sportscover, an international insurance company that specializes in coverage for sporting activities, had developed a calculator that predicted youth injuries based upon factors such as age, sex, and fitness level for many sports. Sportscover rated archery far below even badminton in its rating of the likelihood of an injury occurring for both fit and unfit youths.

So we don't leave people my age out, in 1996, the U.S. Consumer Product

Safety Commission released a report on sports-related injuries for people ages 65 and older. The report lists the 13 sports and activities with the highest number of reported injuries, and archery was not even mentioned.

This is more than a little amazing in that archery is a form of weapons training. How is it that archery has achieved such an admirable safety record?

The most common injury to archers is the string hitting the bow arm. This is preventable!

Well, the answer is that safety is woven into the sport at every level. Here are just a couple of aspects of being safe and running safe programs for coaches. We assume that you have had training regarding archery safety already and, if you have not, this is yet another reason to get certified as an archer instructor or coach.

The Number One Safety Factor

I am going to tell you the "number one archery safety factor" right off the bat (Oops, mixed sport metaphor—sorry!). The penultimate safety factor is *how many students you have per coach*. What this ratio is is kind of a moving target, but let me explain what I mean here.

Take as an example that you are coaching a single student at an outdoor range. The two of you are alone. An accident occurs that requires medical attention ... to you. Your student is not old enough to drive, so he calls 9-1-1. If the range is in an outlying area, you may be in for a long wait.

Or something happens to your archer, let us say you are out on a field range and she is stung by a bee and has a horrific allergic reaction. What are you going to do? We carry small first aid kits while we are with students on field ranges. This, of course, brings up questions of whether you are trained to administer first aid and whether the kit can actually help (in the case of a bee sting allergy reaction, I think not).

I know, I know, when you got into coaching archery you were energized by all the smiles you got from the new archers you were helping to learn archery and you didn't want to think about things like this. This is exactly the reason I am writing this now, so that you will read it, think about, and adopt practices that will leave you with just happy memories of your coaching experience.

This is rule #1: *Never, ever, be alone while coaching.*

You will probably not be surprised that I also recommend that you avoid being alone with underage students of the opposite sex at any time.

On the other hand, you might have a group of 4-5 young students with you and a partner at a range. If an accident were to happen, one of you could arrange for the injured to get treatment while the other cancels the rest of the session. Yes, you read it right – the 3-4 students left behind while your partner is arranging medical help cannot be handled by just one person. Trust me in this, I learned this

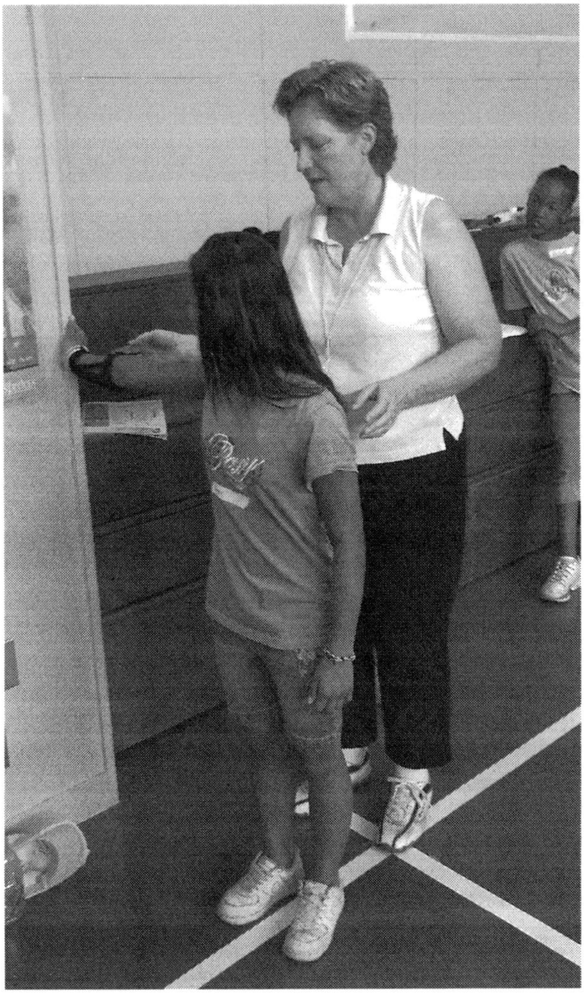

Tp prevent the string hitting the bow arm. the bow hand must be correctly placed on the bow and the elbow rotated out of the way. Here Claudia is showing a young student how to do this.

the hard way. I was on a field range with four adult archers, all of us having fun, when one of them overdrew his bow and shot his own hand. I was very, very lucky that one of the other students was a registered nurse who had her bag in the back of her car. She took care of him, while I walked the rest of the group back to the practice butts where there were other people.

So, how many coaches or coach's helpers does one need? The rule is, if you are working with physically disabled archers, it is 1:1, one coach for each archer and each student-archer should have someone at hand who knows their condition and who can lend aid. Then, generally, for able-bodied archers, the younger the archers, the smaller the ratio. With 8-year olds, maybe 2-3 archers per coach, with experienced teenagers, maybe 8-9 per coach with another adult on hand to lend a hand . . . there always being a minimum of two. We have tried classes for archers under eight, but we also had a lot of coaches, a lot of parents, and an expert in early childhood education as our team. We also decided it was not an appropriate sport for children under eight and we now generally recommend a starting age of eight.

Parents of student-archers often step up and volunteer to be at lessons. There are many things you can have such volunteers help. For example, they can monitor the archers while off the shooting line and other such tasks. This is also one of the ways to identify those we would like to get into a coach training course.

Earning The Right To Shoot

Most departments of motor vehicles will tell you that driving is a privilege, not a right. I think this is a good attitude to take when coaching archers. After the introductory session with new archers, we not so subtly let everyone know this is the case with our lessons. They earn the right to take lessons by showing that they are attentive to, and obedient of, the safety requirements. We tell our students, young and old, that we have three goals for any lesson:

1. That they are safe!
2. That they have fun! and,
3. That they learn something about archery.

Don't Spend Personal Capital

You probably know parents who answer youthful queries with "Because I'm the Mom/Dad, that's why!" Usually this happens when Mom/Dad has had enough and is playing a trump card. What Mom/Dad is doing when she plays the "I'm the Mom/Dad card" is spending personal capital. You must be careful with personal capital, though, because you only have so much of it to spend and, if you spend all of your personal capital, you have no further influence. You probably have met some parents who have no influence whatsoever over their own children. An audit of their personal capital account would reveal a zero or negative balance.

When enforcing safety rules I recommend that you use no personal capital, none, zero, zip. All students need to sign an agreement (or make a pledge, or . . . .) that they will follow all safety rules and instructions (whether written or oral).

I further recommend that you post your rules at the range where you are shooting.

If you have the expectation that your student-athletes will actually follow the rules, you still must teach them the rules and reinforce the rules repeatedly. This is

Archery Range Rules

1. Know and obey all range commands.
2. Keep your arrows in your quiver until you are told to shoot.
3. Always wear your arm guard and finger tab.
4. Only use the arrows the instructor gave you and remember what they look like.
5. Always keep your arrows pointed down or toward the target.
6. If you drop an arrow, leave it on the ground until you are told to get your arrows.
7. Always walk at the archery range.

Archery Range Whistle Commands

Two Blasts "Archers to the Shooting Line."
One Blast "Begin Shooting."
Three Blasts "Walk forward and get your arrows."
Four or More Blasts "Stop shooting immediately! Put your arrows back into your quiver."

Archery Range Procedures

- Stand behind the waiting line until you hear two (2) whistle blasts or "Archers to the shooting line." Take your bow and straddle the shooting line.
- Keep your arrows in your quiver until you hear one (1) whistle blast.
- After you have shot all of your arrows, step back from the shooting line, set your bow on the rack, and wait behind the waiting line.
- After everyone is done shooting and is behind the waiting line, the instructor will blow the whistle three (3) times, then walk forward to the target line.

Pulling Your Arrows

- Two archers at a time from each target may go forward from the target line to pull their arrows.
- Stand to the side of the target and make sure that no one is standing behind your arrows.
- Pull your arrows out, one at a time, and put them into your quiver.
- After you have pulled all of your arrows, return to the waiting line.

Progressive Discipline

true for adults as well as for kids. After they have lived by the rules for some time, you will find that you no longer have to enforce infractions because there aren't any.

To enforce the rules a "progressive discipline" system is recommended. After the rules are explained and an infraction noticed, you cannot ignore it. If you do, no one will take your safety instructions seriously.

Upon a first violation, the infraction is noted, the archer pulled aside (it is no one else's business) and you point out the infraction and the rule (posted) and ask if there was a misunderstanding involved. In most cases you will get an apology.

If there is a second violation of the same or of some other rule, have the archer sit out an end. If it is a group lesson, having to watch the others having fun when they cannot is often persuasive. If a private lesson, taking a 10 minute break from shooting (while still on the clock for a paid lesson) can be persuasive (especially if Mom or Dad is over there giving them "the look").

A third violation merits calling off the session (if just an individual is involved) or taking the bow and arrows away from an archer if he/she is part of a group lesson.

Repeated infractions from lesson to lesson must result in the student being told to find another sport.

We have never had to ask a student to leave, even though we have had more than one or two students who had diagnosed behavioral problems. I believe this system works because all of the student-archers can see the inherent fairness of it and the seriousness of violating commonsensical safety rules. The only way you can mess it up is to play

Please don't climb on the target stands! Thank you.

Please don't climb on the target stands! You will have to sit out one end.

You will be able to shoot again next end if you can agree to follow all of the range rules.

favorites, that is let some archers skate while others get punished. That will destroy any such system.

Don't Be Afraid To Cancel

We have had to cancel group sessions because not enough coaches showed up. If you have a group of students, you need someone to monitor a shooting line, someone to work with an archer from time to time, someone ... it is a long list. You must decide on your student-to-coach ratio and stick to it. We have found that we cannot just take the first six archers and send the others packing. It is always perceived as fair that no one gets to shoot today (disappointing, but fair). We apologize to all profusely and have had parents take us aside and thank us for a valuable lesson being taught their children and for keeping their safety uppermost in our minds.

Insurance For You, Medical Coverage For Them

One of the things we ask of new students is proof of medical insurance. We learned this the hard way. The one and only serious accident we have had over the years happened to a student who was within arm's reach of three adults, in other words, a freak accident. When we got the young man to the hospital, we found out that the woman who had signed the forms (the archer was a minor) was his grandmother and she wasn't sure whether he had insurance or whether her insurance covered her grandson. You must be sure medical treatment can be authorized if needed.

Also, *you* need personal liability coverage. There are many kinds of insurance. The range we were operating at had insurance. The program (JOAD) we were operating under had insurance. And we had our own liability insurance. But, are you familiar with the process of filing a claim? We weren't and we had read the policy! The criteria for filing a claim – do you know them? It is important to 1. Have insurance, and 2. Know the policies.

Because we want to protect ourselves from freak occurrences, we are members of the National Alliance for the Development of Archery (NADA). One of the benefits of NADA membership is two million dollars of liability insurance, usable in case a claim is filed against us personally. Now, I have never heard of such a claim being filed, so I don't want you to get your knickers in a twist, but would you want to bet your home and all of your possessions that such an incident won't occur or would you rather be a NADA member for $40 per year. Guess what we recommend?

We have many, many happy memories about our experiences as coaches and we intend on piling up some more, but like the archery safety rules, there are just some things that need to be done ... just in case.

Being paranoid about safety is a good thing.

What Can I Do?

Things to Do/Read/View

- If you are already part of an archery coaching team, ask about the program's insurance. Ask to see the policy and read through it. This is especially important if you are the program's leader, but protecting yourself is important also.
- Get a copy of the Insight newsletter on safety (www.communityarchery.com/ArcherySafetyInsight.pdf) and read it.
- Make up a set of "range rules" for where your lessons are given. Have it blown up to poster size and laminated so you can post the rules.

3

Tips on Running a Program

Introduction

Most coach trainings don't provide any help when it comes to launching a program. Here are some considerations regarding running a program yourself. It includes pitfalls to avoid as well as foundations upon which you can build a successful program.

It's All You?

Initially any program is identified with its creator, so in the beginning nothing happens without you. In the beginning it *is* all you. But, if it continues that way season after season, you will either get burned out or your program will be lackluster. It takes a team to put on a good program. When Claudia and I started our first program it was just the two of us. But we shortly added volunteer parents and additional (paid) coaches. During the first six years, in which we had as many as five classes a week running (in the summer), we had as many as nine other coaches working. We trained around 25 people to coach for us, quite a few of whom started out as parent-volunteers.

We no longer run that program (we moved away from the area) and the person running it now is one of those parent-volunteers we trained. We also spun off a teenage competitive team by recruiting two coaches. That team is still going strong and we take a great deal of pride in being a part of it.

I can guarantee you that if Claudia and I hadn't reached out to those volunteers and trained those coaches, we would not have gotten very far. Yes, we enjoyed working with the kids but there are many other aspects to running a program that require attention and doing it all yourself quickly wears thin.

If "it is all you," for an extended period of time you will either get burned out or your program will be lackluster. (It was worth repeating.)

It Takes a Village?

Well, a whole village is not needed, but certainly a team is. Let me tell you what the beginning of one of our class sessions was like. We would get to the practice butts of our club, which were reserved for our use by the club (Thank you, Nevada County Sportsmen!) at least 30 minutes early. One of the coaches would be stationed at the equipment shack checking bow fit and handing out bows as the kids came in (some invariably 20 minutes early even though they could not shoot until class had started). Another coach, at another station, would set them up with armguard (required), finger tab (optional), quiver, and properly fit arrows. Bows not in use were required to be on a bow rack (and often the quiver was clipped to the bow). Claudia was greeting incoming students and parents and somebody was working with brand new students of whom, it seemed, there was always one in any class (kids brought relatives, friends, or parents and grandparents who wanted to give it a try). All of the newbies had to get the safety orientation. Somebody else was taking money and getting releases signed by parents. This was for a class of maybe 12-16 young people. Later as we began shooting, newbies got one-on-one coaching—at least through their first few arrows—while other groups of 3-5 were taken out onto the field range and others stayed on the practice butts to work on their form (voluntarily . . . really!).

Now, this I will say over and over—you cannot have a safe program without a reasonable student-coach ratio. And the number of available coach/volunteers starts at two! If we did not have enough coaches to put on a safe class (and we might not know until they didn't show up), we would cancel class. We had disappointed kids and parents, but never one complaint from a parent. Some students warranted a coach dedicated to them alone (some students with physical disabilities, require one coach/volunteer per student). The younger the kids, the lower the student-coach ratio.

I repeated this point even though it was in the safety chapter because it is too important to leave to chance (and some of you might have skipped over that chapter).

Charging and Handling Money

In archery we have this funny attitude that "it's all about the kids" and we shouldn't charge them; it is enough to get them involved in our wonderful sport. This attitude survives in spite of the fact that every other youth sport has substantial fees associated with participation. Check out your local Little League, AYSO Soccer, softball, hockey, tennis, and golf programs to see what they charge. I heard from one parent that their local Little League included an up-front fee (on top of the other fees) to buy the coach a present at the end of the season!

There is paperwork involved!

The reasons you *do* want to charge are numerous. One is the expense of acquiring and maintaining the program equipment. As an example, before one season I did not have time to make replacement bow strings, so I spent $80 out-of-pocket for new recurve bowstrings, even though our local pro shop gave us very good pricing to support us. Straightening arrows, refletching arrows, repairing bowstrings and cables, nocking point locators, etc. take not only time but money. (Buying all of the equipment in the first place is a major expense.)

We checked in with parents from time to time to determine the reasonableness of our fees. One parent said: "Heck, you supply the range, the coaches, the equipment, the insurance, and all we have to do is bring the kids and pick them up. We don't have to sell candy to raise funds or do anything else. This is a bargain!"

Every community has a prevailing price structure, so do check in with the other youth programs as to what they charge. I think you should charge at least as much as the price of a ticket at your local movie theater.

I don't want to beat this to death but when Claudia and I were taking our USA Archery Level 3 Coach Course at the Olympic Training Center in Chula Vista, CA, one of the other coach-candidates told the story that his program was losing students to another youth program. When he finally got to talk to one of the parents of a kid he lost, he asked why the child had dropped out of archery. The parent told him that her child hadn't dropped out but was attending "the other program." He asked (politely) the reason why. Well, the parent said, "You only charge $1 per lesson and they charge $6. . . ." In our culture, the cost of a thing has something to say about its perceived value. So, if you think you have a valuable program, charge accordingly. We have never found a fee so high that people didn't come because of it. But we've never charged as much as other youth programs because we are not in it for the money. But we pay our coaches, we need to be able to cover the costs of purchase, maintenance and repair of equipment, plus the expense of getting coaching certifications and trainings.

Oh, and of course, you must keep records! Open a bank account for just this purpose. Have a sign-in sheet. Mark the sign-in sheet with the amounts paid. Treat your program as equivalent to running a business. If you make a substantial amount of money and don't reinvest it into the program, you may owe taxes. And, if you pay any one coach over $600 per year you are supposed to notify the IRS. Get

advice from other youth leaders as to what they do and from your tax consultant, if you have one.

Equipment Matching

Our first program started with a motley collection of bows and arrows, quivers, armguards and tabs. It wasn't a disaster, but we had a great many problems setting up young archers to shoot. The biggest problem? Nock fit.

If arrows fit too tightly or too loosely on strings, it causes a ton of grief for a new archer. The arrows fall off the bow at full draw! The arrows don't come off the string when shot! What a mess! I was renocking arrows and reserving strings like crazy to get matches.

Arrows were too long, too short, too stiff, etc.

Rather than go on and on, let me tell you what we have now. We now have a "Bow Box" purchased from the National Alliance for the Development of Archery (NADA), paid for, by the way, from fees from archery classes. Bow boxes (*see photos above*) come in various configurations but consist of a large fiberglass case which contains half a dozen to a dozen or more recurve bows and/or Genesis compound bows, quivers, arrows (two sizes, same nocks), armguards, tabs, and tools (nock wrench, bow square, recurve bow stringer). We have gotten as many as 16 bows into our box. The wheels on the Bow Box allow us to get all the gear from our car onto the field quickly and easily. The open box acts as a bow stand. All you need are targets to shoot at on a safe field.

Now, here's the key—everything fits together. The arrows are spined about right and are long enough (or short enough) for kids through adults. The nocks fit the strings, the strings fit the bows, the bows fit the students (draw weights, lengths, etc.). Everything fits! I can't tell you how nice this is! If you are setting up a program, making an investment in matched program equipment is worth it. Give NADA a call and see if they have a Bow Box configuration that works for you.

What to Do During the Sessions

One of the shocks we got when starting up our first program (a USAA JOAD (Junior Olympic Archery Development) program) was that no curriculum was supplied. (As I am writing this book curricula are being developed that give you a structure of what to do on any particular day.) We had no idea of how to structure classes so we started with ordinary targets and balloons and quickly developed other games to play. We had the advantage of the program being placed at a field archery range and the kids (and adults; we had an adult program, too) loved going out on the range.

A key element is to have a fun game or contest saved for near the end of any session. These were often silly, but enjoyable (and safe, of course). At the end of any session (5-week or 6-week) we would have a whole session of contests with prizes. The prizes were inexpensive geegaws we would pick up on our travels. One time we got a whole bunch of stickers and trinkets from the "Spirit Store" at the Chula Vista (CA) Olympic Training Center. When the last trinket was gone, Claudia held up the empty plastic bag and announced "All of the prizes are gone!" The students then started chanting that they wanted to shoot for the bag! And the winner of the bag was overheard later, while showing his kid brother, "Look, it's from the Olympic Training Center!" So, the prizes don't have to be significant

(at least in your mind).

As Good as Any Other Sport

A number of our field club members would grumble that we would put on an archery event attracting over 600 people for a weekend event and get no press coverage. This was true and it may be true for your club or organization. It will no longer be a problem if you run a kid's program as most local newspapers have space in their sports pages for kid's program news. You can also argue that archery is "as good as any other sport" and is an Olympic sport in addition. We were getting front page notice from time to time as well as regular articles about some of our competitive archers, because one of our coaches was willing to send in stories and photos.

Claudia always made it a point to give plaques to coaches at the end of a year as well as make tee-shirts available for sale. We even had cheesy (non-program) medals we would use for strictly fun competitions to train kids how to accept a medal. Kid's medals on their bedroom walls or taken to school provide wonderful advertisements for your program and give it recognition and standing in the community. I was initially worried about how to market our programs, but in the end a simple flier printed from the computer was all we ever used. Newspaper coverage and word of mouth did the rest.

What Can I Do?

Things to Do

- If you are considering running an archery program, create a recordkeeping system to keep track of participants, medical release forms, insurance, the money, and anything else you deem useful. If you, like me, don't like doing these chores, find a team member who can do this for the program.
- In planning for a new program, draw out a diagram showing how a student makes his or her way through a session: they are greeted here, they pay fees here, they get their equipment there, etc. Include who on your team does what, when. A little planning like this can eliminate a lot of confusion due to disorganization as your program runs.
- Uncertain what to charge for sessions? Look up the local movie prices (one benchmark), then contact some of the local youth sports programs (any of baseball, softball, soccer, hockey, golf, tennis, etc.) and see what they charge and how many sessions (practices, games, meetings) that pays for. This should give you a good idea of what the local standard is for charging for organized youth sports. It is up to you whether to charge per session or for a series of sessions, but see what the others do as a guide.
- When you attend archery competitions, keep a notebook with you so you can take notes on suggestions made by other coaches. Archery coaches are generally eager to share the things that make their program special. All you need do is

seek them out and ask about their program.

- If you have no idea what to do for contest prizes, check out your local "dollar store." Fun and unusual prizes can be picked up for a buck or under.

Things to Read/View

There isn't much available advice for running archery programs, so if you can find someone to mentor you, someone who has done this and will spend a little time with you on the phone or at the range.

4

Helping With Equipment

Introduction

I believe there is a major transition point when an archery student buys his own equipment. It is a commitment of a sum of money and also a commitment to the sport. It also marks the line where the equipment can be fully adjusted to the archer. Club or class equipment is fitted to make sure the student has fun and is safe: Are the arrows long enough? Is the bow about the right size and draw weight? . . . etc., Good? Let's go have fun! But when a student is going to purchase equipment, the fit needs to be much better. So, students need help when buying their own equipment. Also, when your students have equipment failures, they will look to you for help.

Buying New Gear

There is an aphorism that says "experience is the best teacher." This is somewhat true. What the aphorism doesn't mention is that the experience can be brutal . . . and expensive. I learned the hard way (through experience) not to just send students off to the wide world of archery merchandise on their own. Even equipped with good advice, students came back to us with equipment that was quite inappropriate for them or for their level of skill. We now try as much as possible to prepare them for the experience. We have a process, called a "bow fitting" which is a separate private lesson lasting an hour to an hour and a half. We assess the archer's skill and then, through discussion and catalog consultation, come up with a written recommendation for the equipment that together we think suits them best. I use a form which I have included here and which you are welcome to copy, modify, use, whatever.

Bowfitting Form

Name of Archer ____________________

Interest in Archery ❒ Recreation ❒ Competition ❒ Hunting ❒ Other

Level ❒ Beginner ❒ Intermediate ❒ Advanced

Type of Bow ❒ Recurve ❒ Compound ❒ Traditional

Style (freestyle, barebow, etc.)

DRAW LENGTH ________ in

DRAW WEIGHT ____ lb

BOW RECOMMENDATION ____________________

OTHER CONSIDERATIONS ____________________

SHOPPING LIST
(*approximate prices may be written in next to item*)

❒ Bow	❒ Arrows	❒ Tab
❒ Bow-Finger sling	❒ Bowstringer	❒ Chest protector
❒ Armguard	❒ Quiver	❒ Sight
❒ Release Aid	❒ Stabilizer	❒ Clicker
❒ Bow Case	❒ ________	❒ ________

OTHER RECOMMENDATIONS ____________________

Fitter ____________________ Date ________

A "bow fitting" starts with some discussion of what the student's long-term interest in archery is: is it bowhunting, target archery (with competition or purely recreational)? Does the archer have a preference for the type of bow? I really insist that students "try before they buy." I will set up a longbow, recurve bow, or compound bow for them to try. (This usually precedes the bow fitting session because of the time it takes.) If I have a suitable loaner, I will lend a student a bow, but you will have to come up with your own ideas of how to do this. The point here is: if a student has never shot a compound bow (or longbow, or recurve bow), how could I possibly fit him for one? Since draw length and draw weight are the critical specifications, it is necessary for you to assess these before making a recommendation.

For Beginners Typically archery students just beginning aren't in the market for archery gear. But, one fall we were besieged by parents and grandparents and aunts and uncles to tell them what to get their little nippers for Christmas (They so loved archery!). Since there were no archery shops within 50 miles, we created a little brochure, listing a wooden-handled recurve bow, a Genesis compound bow, one quiver, one armguard, one tab (different sizes), and Easton Jazz arrows to fit and passed them out. Our living room exploded into an archery shop. We spent weeks building arrows, putting on nock locators, checking shipments, fletching arrows, etc. and arranged to have them picked up in time for the big event.

The point here is that beginners (and their parents, grandparents, aunts, and uncles) do buy gear. The worst case scenario is that they go to a big box store and buy what looks good and the best case scenario is they come to you for advice.

We still recommend wood- or polymer-handled recurves and Genesis compound bows, and Jazz arrows, for people in this situation. The key thing is safe, sturdy, light-weight equipment (both physically and in draw) at minimal cost.

For Archers Past the Beginning Stage Let's assume you know a student who has his heart set on a target recurve bow. How would you go about helping him get what he wants (and at the same time getting him what he needs)? What length bow do they need? What draw weight? If the student is young, he has had a recent growth spurt or you can safely assume he is likely to have one soon. If you recommend a bow that fits him now and six weeks later it is too small, someone is going to be unhappy! Similarly, if you recommend "a size up" for him to "grow into" and he doesn't . . . again someone is going to be unhappy. Since a bow lasts quite a while, assume some growth is involved.

I try to avoid high end equipment when students are still growing. Archers at the point of buying their first equipment do not have settled form. And it is not just a case of a kid growing into a longer draw length, it is a matter of form. As their form improves, things do change. So I try to just move them up a quality/cost ladder, saving the expensive stuff for when they have settled form (and have really committed to the sport).

There are tests to determine draw weight: one such is recommended by former Korean Women's Olympic Coach Kim Hyung Tak of Korea:

Bow Tension Test

Repeat the following sequence: Anchor and extend for seven (7) seconds, and then let down partially for two (2) seconds. If eight or more repetitions can be undertaken easily, the bow tension is fine and the archer can use the (bow); over 12 sets, the archer can use a heavier bow.

You can't always tell from the archer's experience with a program bow. A friend of ours was introduced to archery with a 20-pound recurve (program) bow. She wanted to buy her own bow, so she set her sights on a 22-pound recurve. I tried to talk her into trying a 26-pound bow (as I thought she could handle that) but she was adamant. A couple of days later she was out shooting a 36-pound bow lent to her by a champion archer and . . . she loved it!

Our friend's experience supports our position of: try before you buy! People in archery are very generous and often lend equipment to people on the way up. This provides the opportunity to try out equipment, with your job (as coach) in making sure the equipment is suitable.

If a recurve bow's riser has adjustable limb pockets, draw weight increments can be handled smoothly. Adjustable limb pockets allow for an approximate 10% increase in draw weight from the nominal value. So if your student can handle 26 pounds of draw (at 28 inches), 26 pound limbs can be used. They also can be adjusted to give 28-29 pounds of draw when the limbs are "bottomed out" in the limb pockets. Then 30 pound limbs can be acquired, which can be cranked up to give 32-33 pounds of draw. So, limbs can be purchased in four pound increments for changes while only subjecting the archer to 1-2 pounds of change at any one time. It is a good rule of thumb to not change draw weight more than two pounds at a time so as to not overstress the archer's form.

If your archer wants a compound bow it is even easier to get a suitable draw weight as most bows are adjustable for at least 10-15 pounds of draw weight (typically 15-25% of peak weight). Be sure to recommend a bow at the upper limit of the archer's ability, so draw weight can be lowered by the 10-15 pounds to the archer's accustomed draw weight, then raised as they become stronger archers. Always check the manufacturer's specifications as to the range of draw weights designed into the bow. A good archery pro shop can be a real help here.

Similarly, I recommend that arrows be recommended that are at least one inch or, better, two inches longer than your archer needs. As they grow and get stronger and the draw weight is increased, they need a somewhat stiffer arrow. The two inches "too long" arrow provides the extra length their growth demands and cutting a half or even a full inch off the length of the arrow makes them stiffer. All you need do is order arrows one to two spine groups stiffer than the manufacturer's spine chart suggests to be able to shoot them longer. Again, a good archery pro shop can be a real help with this.

I also provide a checklist including things like tabs, stabilizers, arm guards, quivers, bow cases, etc. so they end up with a shopping list. I indicate an approximate cost for each item and even the manufacturer's suggested retail price if I can find it. (Did I mention I charge for this service?) I then give them a list of shops that I have checked out and who often do well by my students. I also tell them what I expect the shop staff to do to make sure the purchases are correct (checking draw length, etc.).

If you send large numbers of students to a shop, you should expect them to get some kind of break on price and/or service. (Don't expect this to happen automatically; it is a relationship business. Talk to the shop's owner.)

In this fashion, they go shopping armed with a great deal of information and are very much less likely to come back from the shop with unsuitable equipment.

Setting Up

I expect the student to bring her new equipment to her next lesson to get help setting it up. The shop will probably do this, but I have had too many instances of things gone wrong to assume anything. (We once got a brand new compound bow directly from its manufacturer with one cable being 1⅜ inches longer than the other. They were supposed to be exactly the same length.)

Repair Advice and Help

There are all kinds of things I do for my students in the ordinary course of lessons. I will tie on new nocking point locators for them. I will straighten bent aluminum arrows from time to time. (If they bend arrows a lot, I will teach them how to straighten them and then bring my straightener to lessons for them to do their own.) Emergency repairs at tournaments are to be an expected part of your responsibility if you are being paid to coach there. On the next page there is a photo and a list of the things I have with me under these circumstances.

Students often don't know what to do with their equipment, so you may have to write out what you want them to ask a pro shop to do. Be as helpful as you can and try to remember back when you were a "newbie" and didn't know a pile from a peep sight.

Equipment Tuning

This topic is big enough to warrant its own chapter, next.

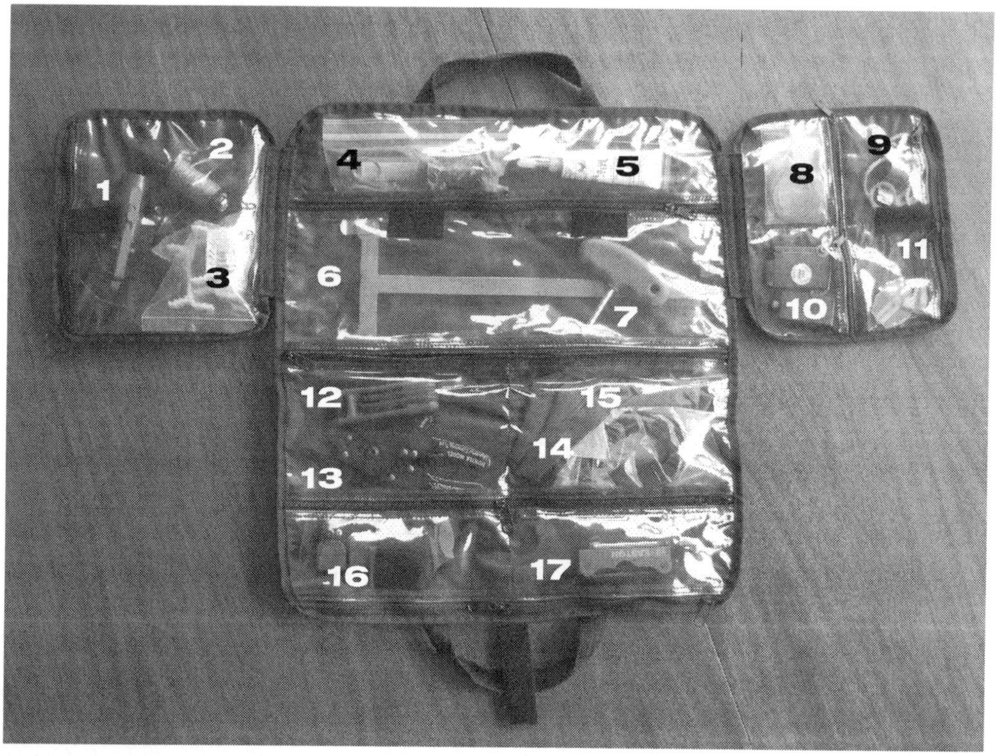

My Coach's Kit

1 Nock Alignment tool
2 Serving tool with braided serving loaded
3 Beiter blocks
4 Serving thread and lighter for tying on nocking point locators
5 Fletching cement
6 Bow square
7 Limb bolt wrench
8 Release rope
9 Metal whistle
10 String and sight levels
11 Various nock wrenches
12 Allen wrenches (English and Metric)
13 Truefire Nocking Pliers
14 Various stretch bands
15 String separation tool
16 Various tabs
17 Easton multitool

The contents of this kit changes all of the time based on new tools that come to me or special situations that students are in. I also have a rather large aluminum tool box full of tools and small parts.

What Can I Do?

Things to Do

- If you are going to be a "bow fitter" create a form similar to the one in this chapter. Get catalogs from your local archery distributors and online sources, if you want to provide cost estimates.
- Check out your local archery pro shop. If you have a relationship with the shop, you may find them willing to give your students special service and even a discount when they bring in one of your forms. If they do this, be sure to "close the loop," and let them know how each transaction worked. (Archery retailing is a relationship business.)
- If you are going to help students with their equipment, you need to be equiped with the proper tools. Acquire a set of basic tools: Allen wrenches, bow square, nocking point pliers, etc. if you don't already have these.
- Make it a point to ask other folks to teach you how to do things you think you need to be able to do (serving a string, repairing arrows, using a bow press, etc.). The book listed below will be very helpful, but finding an "archery angel" (someone who can teach you the skills) is even more helpful.

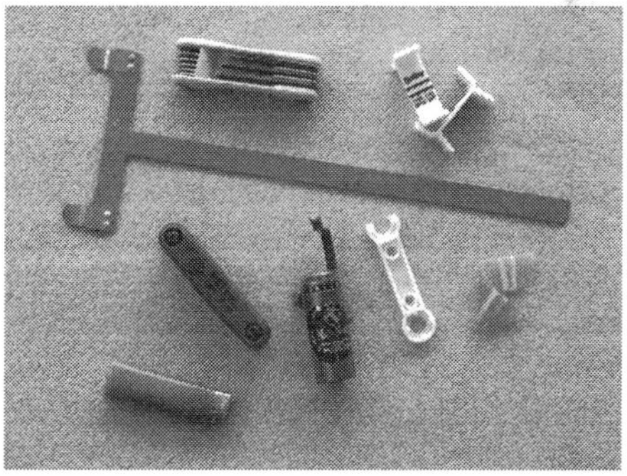

Things to Read/View

There are many, many resources to help you learn about archery equipment, some of them free (see the Resources at the end of this book). The one that is a "must have" for all archery coaches is:

📖 *Simple Maintenance for Archery* by Ruth Rowe and Alan Henderson
Every archery instructor needs a copy of this book! Step-by-step procedures for building arrows, tying on nocking point locators, replacing center servings, etc. (available from *www.qproductsarchery.com*).

5

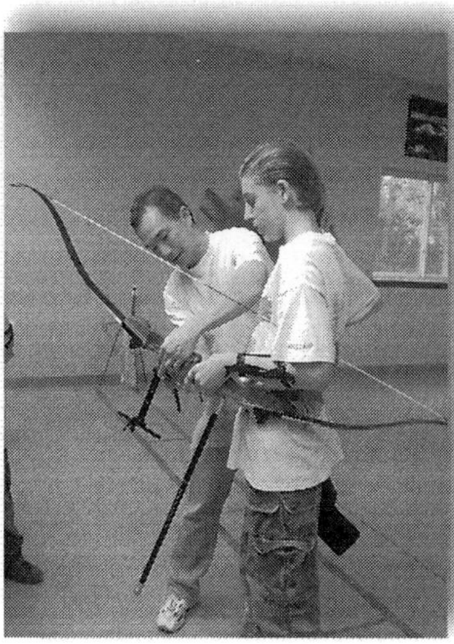

Tuning Concepts

Tuning is the discussion topic of choice of most students of archery, actually of the vast majority of archers, too. There is macro tuning, fine tuning, and micro tuning; there is bare shaft tuning, variable tuning, French (or walkback) tuning, paper tuning, creep tuning, and tuning for groups. There are major segments of archery websites devoted to tuning. So, is tuning the key to being a good archery coach? No.

It is telling that only intermediate archers spend lots of time tuning, much of the time probably misspent. Beginners don't know what tuning is, and elite archers, while they can and do spend considerable time experimenting with equipment, they don't spend a lot of time tuning. So, why are intermediate archers spending (mis-spending?) so much time on tuning? What many are looking for is a magic incantation that will make them shoot better, to not miss, or to beat their competition.

Let's look at tuning, but not from the perspective of an archer learning how to do it. Let's look at it from a coach's perspective. I can't describe all of these methods, so I will just supply you with references in which they are described. (Many of them free! Now, there's a magic word!) We will focus on what you are trying to do, not on how to do it.

What is Tuning?

Tuning is making adjustments in the bow-arrow system to fit them to the archer better. No archer is perfect; each makes mistakes (of aiming, of releasing, of . . .). The goal of tuning is to create a bow-arrow setup that minimizes the impact of those mistakes. Consequently the exact same bow-arrow combination will shoot differently in the hands of different archers. Otherwise all archers need only shoot what

Dave Cousins (compound) or Michele Frangilli (recurve) or the champion archer who is closest to them in size and equipment shoots.

The goal of tuning therefore is a "forgiving" bow-arrow system in the sense that it forgives the archer's mistakes.

Tuning Concepts

Since tuning is such a vast topic, I will not even try to teach you how to do it. For that I refer you to the references at the end of the chapter. I do recommend that you learn as much about tuning as you can. You will have to guide your students through that vast sea of information.

You Can't Tune a Poorly Fit or Poorly Set Up Bow/Arrow

Tuning is just one part of a good bow-arrow-archer system. To get that good system, I break it into three parts:

• bow/arrow fitting
• bow/arrow setup, and
• bow/arrow tuning.

(Realize that all of this technical stuff only goes to support the archer's form—the bow can't shoot itself!)

Bow/Arrow Fitting This step is making sure that the bow and arrows are fit to the archer. The critical factors for the bow are draw weight and draw length. If we are talking about a compound bow, add physical mass to the list. If the bow has too much or too little draw weight, there is no chance you can teach the shooter of that bow good form. Too much draw weight and all the wrong muscles will be engaged in shooting the bow. If too little, they will have trouble getting off of the string. If the draw length is too long or too short, good form is impossible. With recurve bows, this manifests itself (usually) in bow length. Someone under five feet tall trying to shoot a 70 inch recurve bow will find they can't work the limbs sufficiently to get performance out of it. With compound bows, this involves cams, cam modules, and string and cable lengths.

If you are working with a child or an adult with little upper body strength, the mass of a compound bow is also a factor. Holding a 4-6 pound weight at arm's length is an impediment to finding any kind of successful archery form.

With regard to arrows, having arrows suitably spined and long enough is critical to having a forgiving setup. Many students are working with hand-me-down equipment and the arrows are typically overspined. You also need to be sure nock fit (nock on string) is good. (Dad's or Mom's bowstring is typically much thicker than junior's.) There is no way you can "tune in" poorly spined arrows or arrows that are too tight on the string. All you will get is erratic arrow flight.

If the bow and arrows are not suitable to the archer, attempts to tune will be futile.

Bow/Arrow Setup The initial setup of the bow involves setting a starting nocking point position and the centershot of the bow. If you are working with a recurve bow, add brace height to the list. And, if there are accessories: bow sight, stabilizers, clickers, etc., they need to be fitted, too. Since there is such a wide variety of such accessories, we will focus on the adjustments made to the bows and arrows themselves.

You may not know that there are two or three points around which a recurve bow can be tuned. These are typically different brace height settings because if you change anything else, you are either creating a new bow (new limbs, different string, etc.) or you are tuning. A basic principle of tuning is *if you change something and it gets worse, change it back*. This is how we find the optimal bow setup and tune—a little more, a little more, oops, too much! But because there are a number of different points to tune a bow, you want to be sure your basic setup has you near that optimal point you want to find. Consider the following graph (*left*).

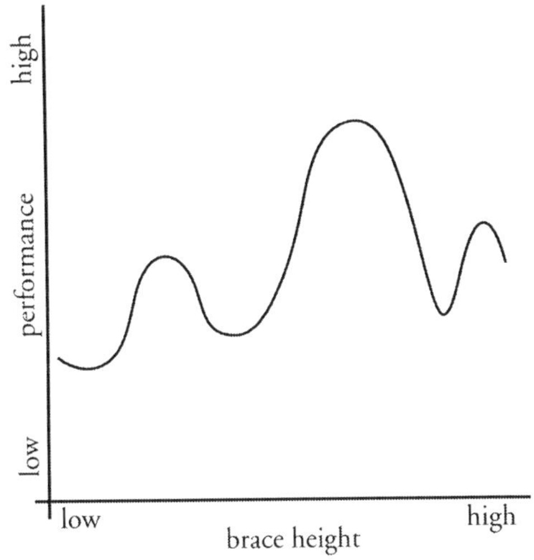

The graph represents the performance of a hypothetical bow (measured by cast or chronograph) as a function of brace height. This bow has three desirable points of tune. The highest peak is the optimal tuning point with the very best performance you can get out of this bow. You want to be sure you are close to the mountain and not just one of hills before you begin any tuning process. Mind you there are very good reasons why you might want to tune on one of the hills, for example shooting short distances indoors, where cast is not so important and a higher brace height may make for a more forgiving setup. But for you and me, either use the bow manufacturer's string and brace height settings or do some brace height tuning before you begin.

Compound bows also can be adjusted for brace height, but that topic is too advanced for this book.

If the bow is not set up well initially, your chances of tuning the bow well are limited. Unfortunately you can tune a bow, well-fitted but slightly poorly set up. You typically end up with a bad tune which means your or your student's equipment is not as forgiving as it could be.

Bow/Arrow Tuning Here is where minor adjustments in the bow-arrow system are made to optimize the setup. These adjustments are in nocking point height and centershot typically and, if a recurve bow, some minor adjustments in brace height). If you are having to adjust draw weight, arrow spine (by cutting arrows shorter or adjusting point weight or vane size). You are really doing bow setup.

Each of these three steps must be done in turn, else the next step is futile.

Step 1 Get a good bow with arrows to match.

Step 2 Set them up near their optimal settings.
Step 3 Tune the bow and arrows.
Some basic practices that apply while tuning are:

You Can't Tune Better Than You Shoot This is probably the source of all of the mis-spent hours tuning. Archers with poor form aren't going to acquire it by going through tuning procedures. If you can't shoot a decent group, tuning the bow probably won't help. In fact, shooting a decent group of arrows is a prerequisite for tuning. (This is why beginners don't tune.)

If You Change Something and It Gets Worse, Change It Back This may seem obvious. It is the basis of all tuning procedures. It is simply the trial and error (trial and test) procedure.

When You Make Adjustments, Make Them Large (At First) Another basic tuning principle is when you make adjustments, make them large (at first). If you are sneaking up an a big problem with itty bitty changes, you are going to be at it a long time. If you are too low, make a big change and now you are too high. Good! You now have a lower limit and an upper limit to your adjustments. Split the difference between those two settings until you get what you want.

Okay, I Lied, So Sue Me

When I started this book I said I was going to teach you not what you needed to *know*, but what you need to *learn*. I am going to keep that promise, but it was felt that some of you might not know what was going on if I didn't describe at least a couple of common tuning procedures. So, here are three common tuning procedures: how to do them and a short section on what kinds of things you can change to make everything as forgiving as possible.

Bare Shaft Tuning

A "bare" shaft is simply an arrow with no fletching on it. When I build up a set of arrows, I typically put nocks and points in the whole dozen but I fletch only 10, leaving me with two "bare" shafts.

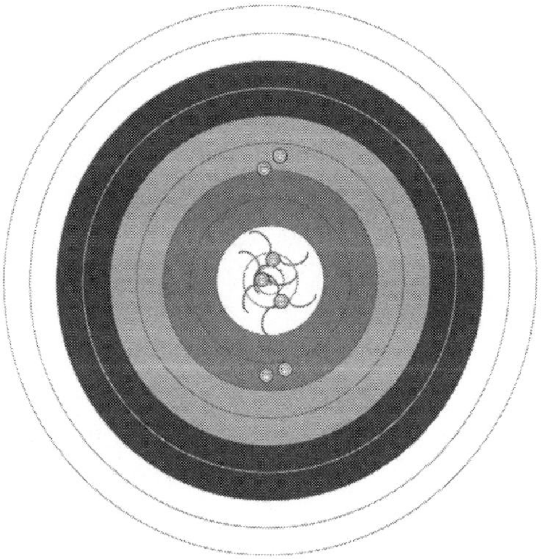

Here's how it goes. Start reasonably close in to a target, 10 yards/meters being a good starting point, although you can expand the distance to as much as 30 yd/m. (But don't start there, if something is really out of whack, you can break an arrow or bare shaft doing this.)

The test is simple: shoot three regular arrows and two bare shafts.

If the three arrows do not make a nice group, start over. The first thing to look for is whether the two bare shafts also form a group, and then where they are. If they are high or low as in this graphic (*bottom left*), you must adjust the nocking point locator to correct for this (move the nocking point locator down if the bare shafts are low and *vice-versa*).

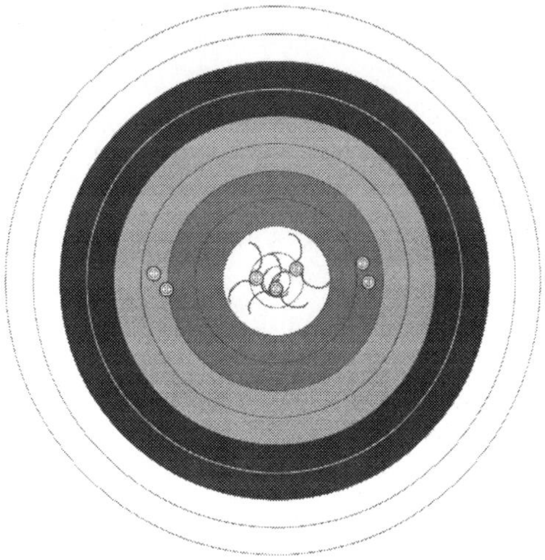

If the bare shafts group and impact to the left or right of the target (*right*), we adjust the centershot (the left-right position of the arrow rest). If the bare shafts group to the left, move the arrow rest to the right, and vice-versa).

Sometimes, no amount of arrow rest change does the trick, or the arrow rest is so far out of normal position that something else has to be wrong. If this is the case, the spine (roughly stiffness) of your arrows is questionable. This is a case of poor set up as getting a bow and arrows to fit you is what set up is all about. But, occasional tweaking of the arrow's spine is necessary. For a right-handed archer, if the bare shafts impact to the left of the fletched arrows, the arrow is said to be "too stiff" or "over-spined". If the bare shafts impact to the right, the arrows are said to be "too weak," or "under-spined." If your student is left-handed, you have to reverse all of the left-rights! Here are some ways you can go about it.

Here are some options to correct a "too stiff" or "over-spined" arrow.

- add point weight
- increase draw weight

And if you have a recurve bow ...

- increase brace height
- decrease number of strands in the bowstring

Here are some options to correct a "too weak," or "under-spined" arrow.

- shorten the shaft (a little at a time)
- reduce point weight
- reduce draw weight

And if you have a recurve bow ...

- decrease brace height
- increase number of strands in the bowstring (or switch to heavier metal nock sets)

Of course you can get combinations of some of these. The general procedure is to handle nocking point location first, then centershot.

French or "Walk Back" Tuning

This method is primarily for recurve archers who use a bow sight. In this method you need a tall stack of bales, or a target mat set on the ground leaning up against another target mat on a stand. Place a small target somewhere near the top of the stack. Start out at about 15 yards/meters, adjust your sight for 15 yards/meters and then do *not* change it! You shoot at the target at the top, walk back five yards/meters before the next shot, and continue until your arrow is impacting at the bottom of the target bale. By looking at the pattern of the arrows, you can determine if the arrows are too stiff, or too weak, or if the centershot needs adjusting (*see the patterns this page*).

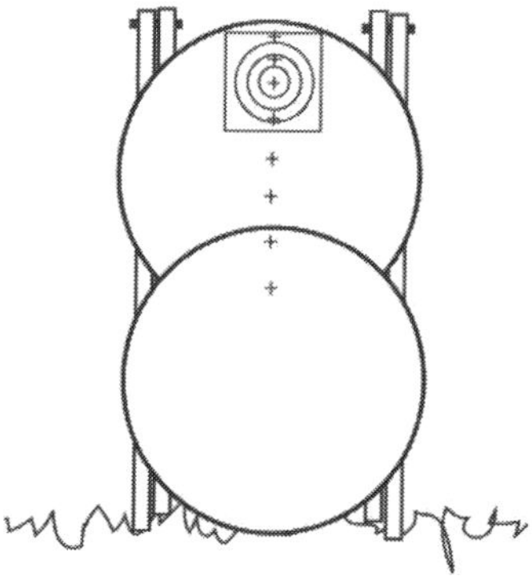

This pattern shows a good tune.

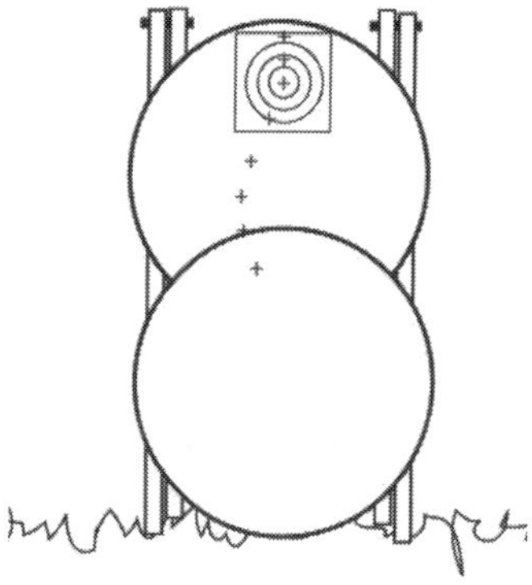

If you get this figure—your rest is too far from the bow (centershot).

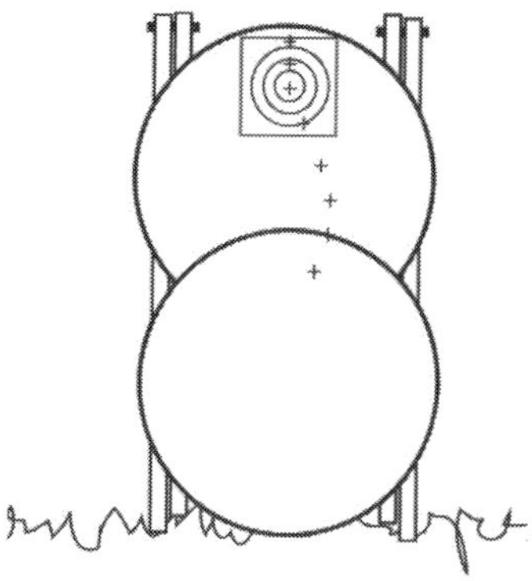

If you get this figure—your rest is not far enough from the bow (centershot).

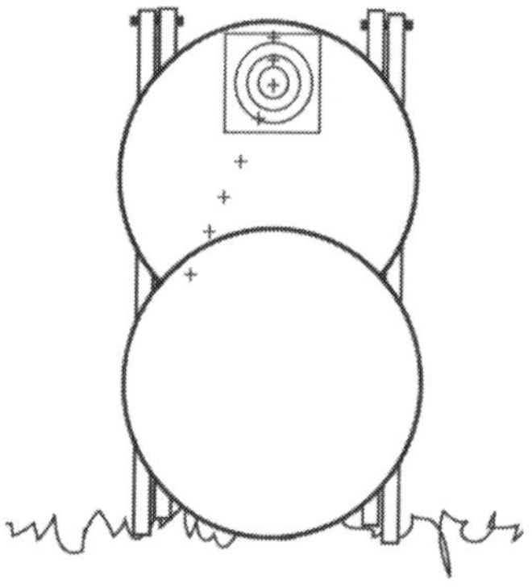

If you get this figure—the side pressure of your rest is too stiff.

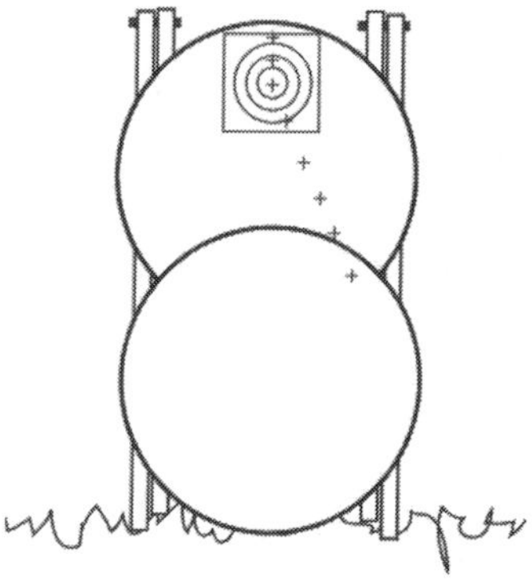

If you get this figure—the side pressure of your rest is too weak.

Group Tuning

This method is easy to describe, but hard to do. It is considered the best of all tuning methods as it tests what we really want to do—shoot high scoring groups of arrows.

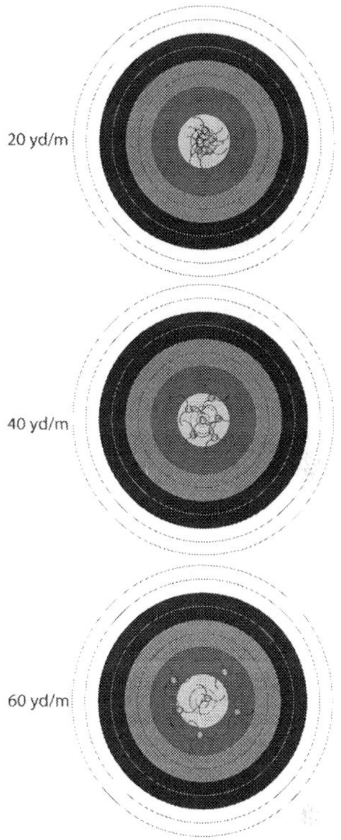

Here's the procedure: shoot groups of 5-6 arrows at different distances. You can shoot pictures of the groups with your cell phone or keep a clipboard with a target drawn on it and mark the locations of all of the arrow impacts. The shapes of the groups should be round and the sizes proportional. That is the group at a distance two times as far should be 2X larger (2X higher, 2X wider), if 3X farther it should be 3X larger (3X higher, 3X wider). Here's a figure to show what I mean (*left*).

The group at 40 yd/m is twice the size of the one at 20 yd/m. The group at 60 yd/m is three times as wide and tall as the one at 20 yd/m. The groups are all roughly round.

Now, here's the hard part. This is a baseline. You then make small changes (in nocking point height, centershot, and rest side pressure—one at a time). And then you test for grouping, generally at the longer distance (long for whatever style of competition, division, etc.). When you get a better group (defined to be still round, but smaller), you test the other distances. (The reason for testing the other distances is you can make changes that make shooting a particular distance better but other distances worse.)

This can take a very long time! So, this is considered something only advanced archers do. That said, I always talk to beginners about knowing what size their groups tend to be. This, I tell them, is a gauge of how well they are shooting. If their groups are getting smaller, they are becoming a better archer. And, everybody has good days and bad days. So, one doesn't compare the size of one's groups with those of other archers, just with one's own. (Well, noting other archer's group sizes does give you some idea of what is possible.)

Tuning Adjustments

I often use the phrase "the bow-arrow system" but it probably should be "the bow-arrow-archer system." The archer's form and execution are a major factor in tuning any bow. As an archer's form and execution changes, so will their bow tune.

I made up some lists of the most common adjustments made in recurve and compound bows and in arrows while tuning. I put them in order of how common they are. But realize that the relative ability to adjust something varies greatly. For example, to increase the spine of an arrow, cutting anything off of the length of the shaft outweighs all of the other changes combined. This is why you must be very careful cutting arrows. Cut them too short, and there is very little you can do to fix that mistake. Other adjustments are more proportional.

Recurve Adjustments
- nocking point location (up-down)
- centershot location (in-out)
- adjusting rest side tension
- brace height (adjusted by string length)
- placement of stabilizer weights (usually done by group testing)

Compound Adjustments
- nocking point location (up-down)
- centershot location (in-out)
- draw weight adjustments (done by screwing limb bolts in or out)
- adjusting launcher rest tension
- placement of stabilizer weights (usually done by group testing)

Arrow Adjustments
- adjusting shaft length
- adjusting point weight
- nock indexing to address clearance problems (rotating nocks to new position)
- adjusting rear end weight (usually done by adjusting fletching size, composition)

Do yourself a favor an get one of the better tuning books and keep it on your bookshelf for reference.

Helping Your Students Tune

Your job as a coach is to provide direction regarding fitting, setup, and tuning. If you want your student as a partner (always a good thing in my book) you will have to explain some of the concepts above. All issues regarding fit must be addressed before setup, which must be addressed before tuning. You must help choose a tuning method when you get to it, one that is within the shooting ability of your student and one that can be done easily and fairly quickly.

You will also have to deal with, well, it usually goes something like this:

Student "I was talking with Bruce and he said paper tuning is the only . . . , etc., etc."

Be sure to hear your student out. Explain the pros and cons of that particular method . . . and let the student choose. If you are not set up to doing paper tuning (or whatever), you could send him to a nearby pro shop. But you should explain that the pro shop's staff wasn't put on the planet to play with them. There is an expectation that some business will come the shop's way (eventually) and that the shop is not to be taken for granted.

Your most important task is to eventually say "enough." Archers can become obsessed with tuning (as all archers believe in magic) and there is a point where too much emphasis is put on tuning. You will probably have to redirect your student's energies away from tuning at some point and on to more productive efforts (like practicing well).

What Can I Do?

Things to Read/View

If I had to recommend just two books to you on this topic (one for recurve, one for compound) they would be the two following. But, there are many, many more available (see end of book).

- *Tuning Your Compound Bow*, 4th Edition by Larry Wise
  Great little book from a master coach and archer! The first and the last word on tuning compound bows. (available from Target Communications, *www.deerinfo.com*)
- *Handbook of Modern Recurve Tuning – Start to Finish* by Richard Cockrell While a little rough around the edges, you would be hard pressed to find a more comprehensive guide to tuning recurve bows. The only ones I know selling it are USA Archery (*www.usarchery.org*) and Lancaster Archery (*www.lancasterarchery.com*).

Things to Do

- If you have some spare time and like to hang around, ask your pro shop's bow mechanic if you can watch him work. I learned a great deal this way.
- If you encounter someone expert in the workings of bows, ask if you can help/observe. Some of the best bow mechanics around don't have that in their job descriptions. You pay for your instruction by being helpful.

Photo Courtesy of Miles Ross

6

The Mental Side of Archery

Introduction

Since this book is directed at coaches of beginning to intermediate archers, you may be wondering why there is a chapter on mental skills. Isn't that for the better archers, the elite archers? And, don't you need to be a psychologist or something? The short answers – no and no. We are not talking about sports psychology, *per se*. We are talking about performing. Performing on the archery field, in school, at work, in play. We are not talking about mental problems, but about the ways ordinary people think. Also, very, very few of the archers you coach will go on to become advanced archers, even fewer to become elite archers, but the mental skills learned along the way aren't just archery skills, they are life skills, too. This may be the most important chapter in this book if you consider the "success" of your students to be more than just first, second, and third places.

Archery is a reflective sport. Everything an archer does affects his shots. The target, therefore, is a record of what that archer was doing and *thinking while doing it*. So, you can't teach archery without also teaching mental skills. As Don Rabska says, "The bow teaches us everything we need to know, if we can just learn to listen to it."

In this chapter we will just be scratching the surface so, if you want to get better as a coach, you will have to accept the challenge to learn as much as you can about the mental side of archery and pass it on to your students.

Being of Two Minds

All that you will hear or read about the subject of archery's mental side will mention two minds – the conscious mind and the subconscious mind. Each of us has these two minds and, if we don't, it sure seems like we do! Since no one knows exactly what a mind is this is easy to say, hard to explain. I assume you know what I am talking about so far.

It is an axiom that "change is hard." It is hard for archers. It is hard for old people, young people, dogs, goats, you name it. It is hard because to learn something new you must go through your conscious mind and think about what you are doing. Do you remember learning to drive? Learning to hit a baseball? To knit? To play the piano? Trying to rub your stomach while patting your head? It is always a struggle at first. Everything is laborious because it must be thought out before and during the activity. You would exhaust yourself very quickly if you had to consciously think your way through a single day. Just brushing your teeth would wear you out.

So, what are you thinking about while brushing your teeth? Well, anything but thinking about brushing your teeth! So, how is it we can accomplish "brushing our teeth" without thought? It is because you trained yourself, actually you trained your subconscious mind, to do it for you. Your true power comes through your subconscious mind. This is how you accomplish 99% of the tasks you have in any given day. Your subconscious mind has almost inexhaustible resources to take care of what you train it to do. It accomplishes these things effortlessly. Your subconscious mind is capable of executing near-flawless archery shots. Your conscious mind is only capable of training your conscious mind. No one can shoot well consciously. So, it is easy, no? Just use your conscious mind to train the unconscious and we are home free, right? Well, as most things in life, it is not that easy.

Training the Subconscious

Your subconscious mind is trained through repetition. The ancient Greeks knew this as they recognized that "Repetition is the mother of learning." But can you actually repeat any physical activity exactly? The short answer—no. But the closer you come to repeating the exact same activity, the more quickly the subconscious will be clued in and take over.

And herein lies one of the great values of a coach (archery or other). A coach can help you get to the point where you are doing things correctly fairly quickly. From then on you are training your subconscious mind to do things correctly. Without a coach, you can end up practicing doing things incorrectly and then spend a lot of time drilling that incorrect behavior into your subconscious mind. Then the only way to correct that mistake is by even more practice doing things correctly. The sooner an archer can get to some approximation of good form, the sooner he or she will be training his subconscious mind to do what is really needed.

Your conscious mind has limitations the subconscious mind doesn't. Your conscious mind can really only focus on one thing at a time, while your subconscious is a fabulous multi-tasker. The "Nine Steps to the Ten Ring" is an attempt to break down what is ideally a single activity, the archery shot, into bits that can be practiced one at a time until relegated to subconscious control. This is typical of other sports, too. How many parts do you think a golf swing has? Or a swing of a baseball bat? This limitation of the conscious mind virtually requires this. The activity—the shot, the swing, the free throw—is repeated over and over, with the conscious mind directed at just one part in an attempt to change that part for the better.

You will hear arguments about "the correct number of parts" to break down an archery shot. This is silly. All of the parts will be combined into one in the end. Some people prefer more parts, others fewer. Your job as a coach is not to insist on a "correct number" of parts, but that only one part can be practiced consciously at a time. An archery shot then becomes a flowing sequence of steps the archer thinks about one at a time, then dropping each thought as he or she moves to the next phase of the shot.

Practice Consciously, Shoot Subconsciously

So far, it sure sounds like "Just use your conscious mind to train the unconscious and we are home free." Well, yes, so far. But there are problems. Other major limitations exist in both minds. The subconscious mind allows us to do vastly complicated tasks with almost no energy output. Its weakness is it is always looking to save even more energy. This is critical to our existence. If we need less energy to survive, we will survive longer! But it is a real problem with repetitive actions. Every time you execute an archery shot a little differently, your subconscious mind evaluates whether that particular shot took less energy and whether the outcome was acceptable. I can remember when I was learning to shoot a release aid and while I was drawing my bow I triggered the release by bumping my chin. Some of these

arrows scored well. My subconscious mind feasted on those shots because that was a lot easier than achieving full anchor, settling, holding, and pulling through the shot. That lucky shot was worth more to my subconscious mind than ten shots executed correctly.

The subconscious mind is always looking for short cuts. Which means you have to keep training it to perform the way you want or it will drift off looking for energy efficiency. A practical implication of unfocused practice is that it is not just a waste of time, it is detrimental to performance by training the subconscious to do other than you really desire.

The conscious mind has a very big limitation. It can only think about one thing at a time, but it has to have that one thing. If it doesn't have a bone to gnaw on, it will inject itself where it isn't needed. While shooting, archers have to give their conscious minds something to focus on or they will start thinking about some part of the shot, or worrying about how the arrow will score, or how they will place in the competition, or.... In other words, you can't let your mind drift off, like you can while brushing your teeth. You must be focused. This is why in a shot sequence there is something to think about (consciously) along with each thing to do.

In the Practice chapter and in other places I will discuss the "one next thing" concept of practice, which is a natural outgrowth of the conscious mind training the subconscious and only being able to focus on one thing at a time.

As a coach, do you think this comes naturally to your archers? No? In my opinion, nothing about archery is "natural;" it all has to be learned. And, if it can be learned, it can be taught. Coaches are teachers and much of what you have to teach is about the mental side of archery.

Isn't That Just Like Me?

There is one more aspect of the mental side of archery that must be touched on to complete the picture, so to speak. We all have a "picture" of who we are inside. (It isn't at all accurate – my picture of myself has me at only about half of my chronological age.) This is what Lanny Bassham and others refer to as your "self-image." The thing is that we protect that image. If we are performing at a sub par level, we bear down and perform better, to agree with that self-image. If we seem to be succeeding beyond our wildest dreams, we flub up and "come back to ourselves." There seems to be a "zone" where we are comfortable with our performance—a *comfort zone*. If we are out of our comfort zone on the high side, we have a slip up or mistake that brings us back into "our" zone. If we are out of it on the low side, we put out a better effort and raise our performance into "our" zone. If we are way out of our comfort zone on the low side, we will dismiss the experience as being meaningless or, as my younger students say, "It's stupid!" So, if we want to perform better we have to make our "self-image" a better one to allow it. We have to expand our comfort zone to allow for better performances.

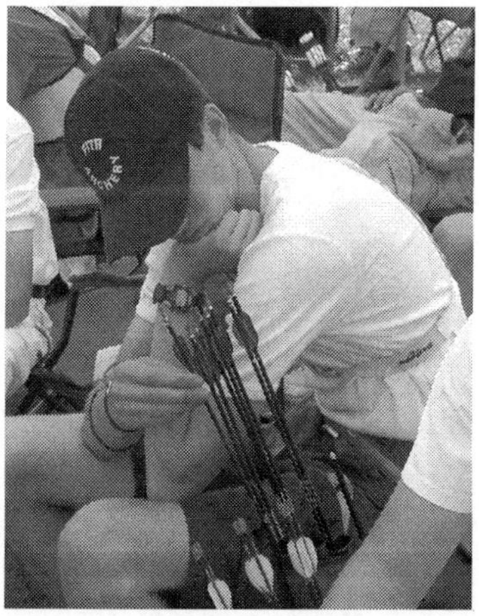

I can remember distinctly when I was pursuing a perfect score of 300 on the NFAA indoor round—60 arrows at 20 yards. I shot in the 280s for years, then I learned a few things and then shot in the 290s. I had one sequence of rounds (shot on different days) that went 294, 295, 296, 296, 297, 298, and 299. Guess what the next score was. If you guessed 298, you guessed correctly. I then used every mental skill at my command to shoot a perfect 300. The next round I shot after I had that breakthrough—284! I remember being relieved when I missed! My self-image did not include me being an archer who got perfect scores.

So, how do you convince yourself that you *are* different? The only way you can do this is ... by *being* different! So if you want to shoot perfect scores, you have to become comfortable doing it. You have to accept that you have such scores within you. The secret to doing this is no secret—it is the same way we start out young archers, with early success. We start out with a big target up really close. Take a 48 inch (122 cm) target and put it up no more than 10 yards/meters away. Shoot 30 arrows in ends of three. Don't settle for mere 10s. Shoot for the X ring! Shoot for the molecules inside the X! If you can't shoot a perfect score, move the target closer. Shoot this round several times. Accept nothing less than a perfect score. Then move the target back one or two yards/meters. Shoot several perfect scores in a row. Move the target back. After several weeks of this, switch to a smaller target (moved closer if you can't maintain those perfect scores). The goal is a regulation-sized target at regulation distance. What you are really doing is accustoming your mind to the fact that you are someone who shoots perfect scores. It is "normal" for you. It is part of who you are!

Now this practice routine is perfect for serious beginners or for committed, dedicated, "seasoned" archers, but it would be stupid if the goal weren't attainable. Shooting a perfect FITA round score at 90 meters is not a reasonable goal. But the idea is still good. Why practice anything but hitting what you are aiming at?

Old school coaches think this is mollycoddling. They will say things like, "You need to get used to missing." "It will toughen you up!" "Aiming at a really small target will help you aim!" By this logic, practicing striking out will help you as a baseball player and trying to catch passes thrown way out of your reach is good practice for football players.

Always start with success, then build on it.

Coaching Self-image

All young archers I coach want to shoot long shots—70 yards/meters and up. With a 15-pound draw recurve bow, this is about a par three—shoot; go pick up your arrow and shoot again; go pick up your arrow, shoot and (maybe) hit the target. There is something about the beauty of a long shot arcing through the air that transcends whether the arrow hits its target or not. I don't want to drive out the fun from archery ... but, if I have a serious archer, young or old, I am helping develop his self-image from day one. And that *doesn't* include long shots (except for an occasional eruption of, well, fun).

Many young archers have grossly inflated ideas of who they are. They have been overly praised for mediocre work. They have gotten A's in school for work barely above average. Every sports team they have been on resulted in them winning a trophy because everyone gets a trophy nowadays.

Others are at the opposite end of the spectrum. They have been told they are incompetent, will never amount to anything, and given no praise for quality efforts.

Most young archers are in between these extremes, but you will see them all.

These out-of-balance self-images will not magically be corrected under your tutelage, but you can help. Giving praise for effort, not results, is a key. So is letting scores speak for themselves. Both Claudia and I were not prepared when we first started working with children. Youngsters would burst into tears when they would fail to reach a qualifying score for a next level of achievement. We even had students pleading with us to award them a new ranking when their scores fell "just a few points short." Scores are very meaningful to young people, something we expect to change with maturity, and allowing students to hedge their accomplishments is very destructive to a healthy self-image. They will always know they didn't earn the award you give them, if you give in to wheedling, begging, or pleading. Self-image and self-esteem are built on a foundation of honest accomplishment. Archery allows young people to see their accomplishments without the interpretations of their elders. They can see the arrows sticking in the target (or not).

Help them see themselves, literally. Videoing them over time lets them see their improvement, lets them see their form, and helps them form a self-image of who they are as an archer, again without the interpretations of their elders (or peers).

Coaching the Mental Side of Archery

As a coach, you must be unfailingly positive to help students, young and old, to bolster their self-images. Focusing on needed changes always sounds negative: Don't pluck the string! Don't drop your bow arm! Don't arch your back! Next time, don't cant your bow! and this needs to be balanced with positive feedback. USA Archery recommended the "Oreo Technique." In this technique, every request for change (the crème of the cookie) is sandwiched between two positive comments (the cookies). Here is an example: For an archer dropping his bow arm during the shot, this might be the comment:

(*cookie*) You had a good release on that last shot, Hal.

(*crème*) What I would like to see is your bow arm held very steady after your release.

(*cookie*) And I hope you noticed how much smaller your groups have gotten with practice.

It is a little cumbersome, but it ensures that the positive comments outnumber the requests for change (usually perceived as negative) by two to one. Also note that the request for change is delivered in a positive manner ("what I would like to see is your bow arm held very steady" instead of "don't drop your bow arm"). *Always describe what you want to happen*, not what is too be avoided. The classic example of this is the young baseball player who is sent to the plate (bottom of the ninth inning, two outs, etc. etc.) with the instruction "Whatever you do, don't strike out!" Just what is he supposed to do and how is he supposed to do it? A positive instruction like "Get a hit!" or "Keep your eye on the ball!" is eversomuch more helpful.

Learn all you can about the mental side of sports. Read books. Attend seminars. Watch videos. Please look at some of the recommended references. Get feedback from other coaches and your students on how well you stay positive when commenting on your student's archery. Realize that you will have an impact no matter what you do and, like archery, coaching is learned, it doesn't come naturally.

What About Sport Psychology?

You may have noticed that I haven't really said anything about sport psychology. There are reasons I have not. First, what I have been talking about is called performance enhancement, which I believe is the proper topic. Second, it is highly unlikely that any of us will learn enough sport psychology to be able to use it (whole degrees are offered in the subject). If you want to have a go at it, let me know how it worked out.

If you have a student who has a serious mental condition affecting their ability to shoot and enjoy archery, talk to the athlete and his/her parents about seeking advice from a fully qualified sport psychologist.

Personally, I don't think this will come up very often.

What Can I Do?

Things to Do

- If you are an archer (You are, aren't you? You aren't letting them have all the fun, are you?) use your own participation to investigate mental programs. The book listed below explains many of the things you need to incorporate in a mental program for your own archery. Then, when you recommend such things to your students, they will have the "ring of truth" in their ears.
- If you are involved in a significant way in another sport (golf, tennis, pistol shooting, etc.) check out what that sport offers in the way of mental skills. My experience is that there are many similarities between golf and archery, for example. (The current focus on this topic in the general public got started with a book called "The Inner Game of Tennis.")
- Go to *www.mentalmanagement.com* and sign up for their free newsletter. There is useful information in each issue as well as a calendar of seminars and events, all dealing with Lanny Bassham's mental teachings.

Things to Read/View

There is a whole lot available for this topic. See the end of book resources; for now the "must read" book for the mental game is:

- *With Winning in Mind* by Lanny Bassham (available at *www.lannybassham.com*) This is an absolute "must have" for any archery (or other) coach who wants to understand the mental game. Over 100,000 copies sold!

7

Practice

Introduction

This chapter is about practice ... and a lot more. Mostly it is about the structure of your work as a coach. Much coaching takes place during practice sessions, some takes place at tournaments, and some takes place at other times in unusual circumstances. Do you know what it is you want to teach? Even though you may be being consulted for one major reason (tournament preparation, teaching new archers how to shoot, helping an archer with bow setup and preparation or in acquiring better equipment), there are other things that should be in your mind. The concept of "Athletes First, Winning Second," a philosophy of helping athletes to become better people as well as better performers, has much to recommend it. The concepts of safety and sportsmanship should never take a back seat to technical matters or winning.

Introductory Sessions / Getting to Know You

Your first meeting with your athlete is an important one whether you are working one-on-one with a seasoned competitor or having your first meeting with a group of young people having their first archery lesson. Let's look at these in turn.

Meeting With a Group of Newbies Let's say you are meeting with a group of young archers (JOAD, 4-H, NASP, church, club, etc.) getting together for their first archery lesson with you. In this situation there is very little you can take for granted. I have had students so excited about hitting the gold during their first lesson that they started to run to the target to look at it. (It helps to have long arms and a loud whistle.) This obviously isn't going to happen with seasoned archers. Your task with beginners is to get them participating—safely—as soon as is possible. Your goals for such archers in a first session might be:

1. acknowledgement of and compliance with all basic archery safety rules,
2. experience success, and
3. have fun!

These beginners, youth or adult, expect you to structure their lessons and set the goals. They do not know enough about archery to even participate in decision making. We will address a model curriculum for beginners shortly. Your job is to get the relationship off on the right foot. In just a few lessons, you have to establish the ground rules for participation in your program. All of the relationships are just beginning, so leave nothing out. Obviously this must be communicated carefully so be sure to read the section on communication below.

Communication is not easy. What happens when anyone gives a safety lesson *as a lecture* to a group of young people, is they get various forms of inattention for their effort. It is really hard to listen to someone go on and on when all you really want to do is to shoot some arrows.

We developed the following procedures to address this problem. We teach each new archer his or her first three arrows face to face, one on one. We have started to introduce safety rules when we passed out their equipment (no "dry fires", arrows stay in the quiver except on the shooting line, etc.). While we have their full attention helping them to shoot their first three arrows, we slip in a few more safety instructions (you have to be on the shooting line so you can't shoot anybody, the arrow always points at the target, etc.). After they have all shot their first three arrows we walk to the target (We always walk on the archery range!) and we then teach them how to pull their first three arrows (face to face, one on one). By the end of the session they have each gotten personalized instruction (Are you behind the waiting line, Jaime?) on the safety rules (including the whistle system and where the rules are posted).

Meeting With Committed Archers A very different meeting takes place when you take on serious archers. This meeting is usually one-on-one or one-on-two if you are working with shooting partners or a parent may be involved if the student is young. This may be a "talk only" meeting but more than likely would involve you observing the student shooting and doing an assessment. At this meeting you would want to get answers to a number of questions:

1. Do you both feel the relationship is worthwhile enough for there to be a commitment to lessons?
2. What are the goals for these lessons?
3. When will the lessons take place, where, how much will be charged, etc.
4. How will you both know the lessons have been successful?

This last question is a tough one to answer, it might be just the personal satisfaction of the participants or it might be a certain national ranking based on competitive performances. I think some time needs to be spent at least talking about this because the other questions could be answered satisfactorily, but there could still be an unrealistic goal in the student's mind.

Working With Individuals

With single students, in a group or not, there is a structure that can support your teaching and their learning. It is called the "One Next Thing" system. It is based on the principles of "practice is conscious, performance is (largely) subconscious" and "you can only think about one thing at a time." During a competition you want your archer focused on what they can do to create a good score. This means a mental program focused on the feel of the shot with the conscious mind doing as little as possible. But during practice, it takes conscious thinking to train the unconscious mind to do what you want and the conscious mind can only do one thing at a time. There are people who say they can do several things at once, that is they can "multitask." Multitasking is doing a number of things in the same time interval, but by switching back and forth between them, so it is a really rare individual who can do two things at once. (Which is why "rub your stomach and pat your head" is such a challenge for school children.)

So, when a student, wanting to improve, asks you what they should do next, you can assess what they are doing and, even if you find three things they need to work on, you only give them their "one next thing." Before they are given another thing to work on, they need to demonstrate progress on the previous "one next thing." This practice prevents the student from drifting from one thing to another during practice and not making any real progress. It also provides a structure for the relationship between coach and athlete. The athlete asks for a "one next thing" and then needs to demonstrate progress on the last thing they were working on. This puts the athlete somewhat in charge of their own training and progress. Of course, the coach can make suggestions along the way. And it puts the student in a position of being receptive to coaching because they are asking for it. When the coach assesses the progress and finds it sufficient, it creates a positive progress that the student can be proud of.

There are a couple of things the coach needs to be constantly focused on:

1. *All of the parts of the archery shot need to be improved together.* It makes no sense to have a world-class stance and a beginner's pluck for a release. Improvements are incremental. This gives everyone an impression that improvements are being made. Don't wait for something to be perfect to move on; reward progress and head to the "one next thing."

2. *A shot sequence provides a good framework for making suggestions of a One Next Thing.* What's a shot sequence? It is just a breaking down of an archery shot into a series of arbitrary phases that allows you and your students to pay attention to any phase that needs work. Possibly the most famous archery shot sequence in the U.S. is the "Nine Steps to the Ten Ring," the steps of which are:

1. Take your stance,
2. Nock an arrow,
3. Set your hands,

4. Raise the bow,
5. Draw,
6. Find Your Anchor,
7. Aim,
8. Release the string, and
9. Follow through (*see graphic right and next two pages*).

These are not necessarily separate activities, but are always points in the process to focus attention. Some people have as few as four steps, others have many more than nine.

When your assessment of a student results in a long list of deficiencies, working your way through a standard shot sequence, like the "Nine Steps" gives you a structure for the process. So, if among all of the things needing correction, the stance is flawed, fix that first, and so forth. This not only provides some structure as to what to do first, second, etc., but if an earlier step is flawed, it will just require a later step to be messed up to make things work, so it has the logic of "first things first." Of course, keeping notes is important so that you can always be aware of where any particular archer stands.

3. *Students sometimes get stale working on a single aspect of their shot.* If your student gets bored with the exercises you recommend (or possibly you are having difficulty giving them exercises that work) move on! Go to something else. It is not a problem. Students getting bored and detached from the process is a problem! If some aspect of your student's shot is clearly a bottleneck to their progress as a whole, then skipping over it is unlikely to produce any progress, and your job is tougher. Ask around to other coaches to find new and novel ways to keep your archer working on that flaw in her shot. Check in with your student to see if something outside of archery is causing the problem. Whatever is the case, find some way to enjoy the practice. The phrase, "It is supposed to be fun!" is true.

4. *Things normally get worse before they get better.* Most beginners make incredible progress . . . in the beginning. As they mature, progress is harder to find. A golfer who breaks 100, then 90 is very excited. Breaking 80 is cause for celebration! But don't expect to break 70, 60, 50, 40 etc. any time soon. Very few golfers have ever broken a score of 60 for 18 holes and very few ever will. Theoretically the minimum score is 18—eighteen consecutive "holes in one," but each of the 500-yard holes is going to require one heck of a tee shot!

The same is true in archery: for a 300 round, the last 10 points are extremely difficult to get.

So, students start out with extraordinary success, then that levels off, then you talk them into a form change and their scores go down! (Nobody likes it when their scores go down!) Students have to be taught to expect this. The new, not quite well-trained procedure is not as good as the old, well-trained procedure . . . but it has the capacity to be much better when it gets to be a new, well-trained procedure.

The Nine Steps to the Ten Ring

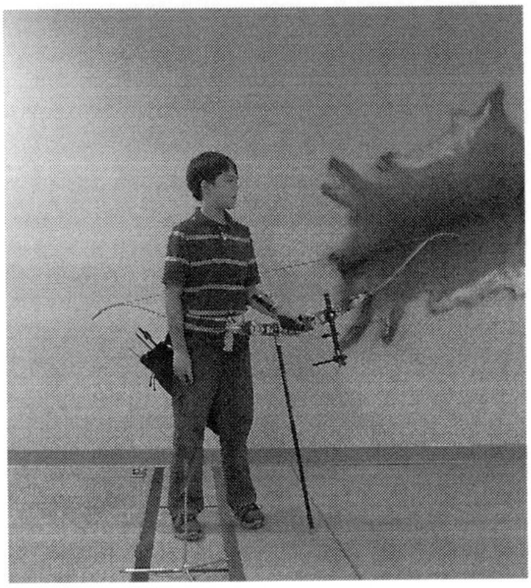

1. Take Your Stance

- Feet spread about shoulder width
- Feet straddle shooting line
- Feet in the same spot every shot
- Weight evenly distributed
- Relax

2. Nock an Arrow

- Cock vane out
- Listen for snap of nock
- Arrow on rest
- Arrow under clicker (if used)

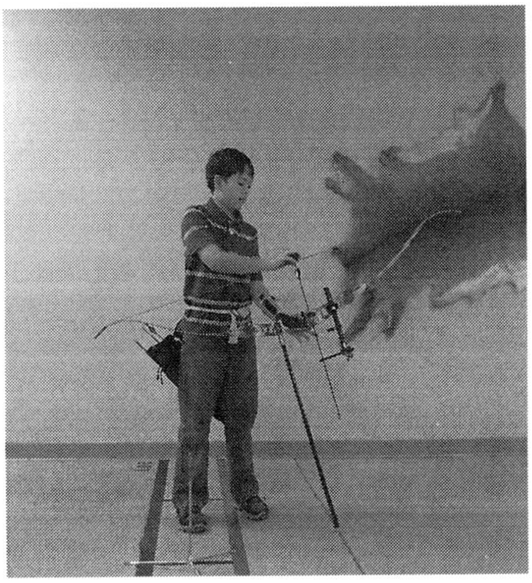

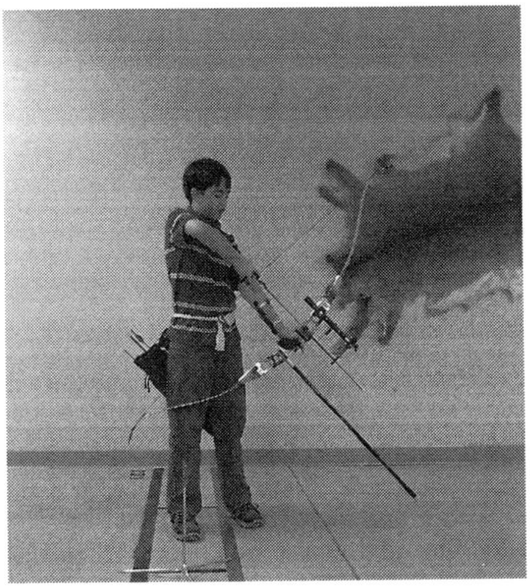

3. Set Your Hands

Bow Hand

- Bow on pad of thumb
- Knuckles at 45°

Draw Hand

- Deep hook
- Hand and wrist relaxed
- Thumb and pinky tucked away
- Relax

4. Raise the Bow

- Bow shoulder stays down
- Bow elbow rotated out
- Draw elbow up
- Hands stay put
- Sight aperture slightly above target (if sight used)
- Relax

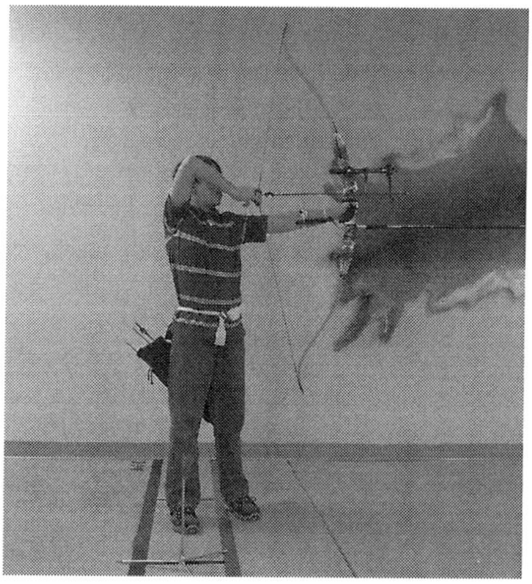

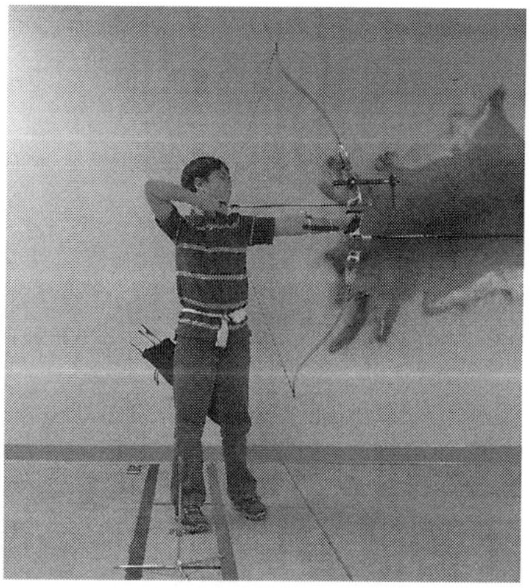

5. Draw

- Pull is smooth and crisp
- Elbow up
- Back starts to work

6. Find Your Anchor

- Keep head still
- Thumb under jaw (low anchor)

or

- Index finger under cheek (high anchor)
- String visible in aiming eye
- String touches tip of nose (low anchor)
- Press the flesh (firm contact at anchor)

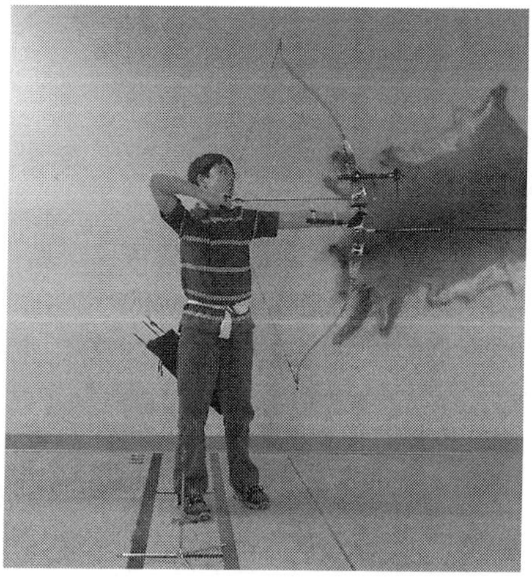

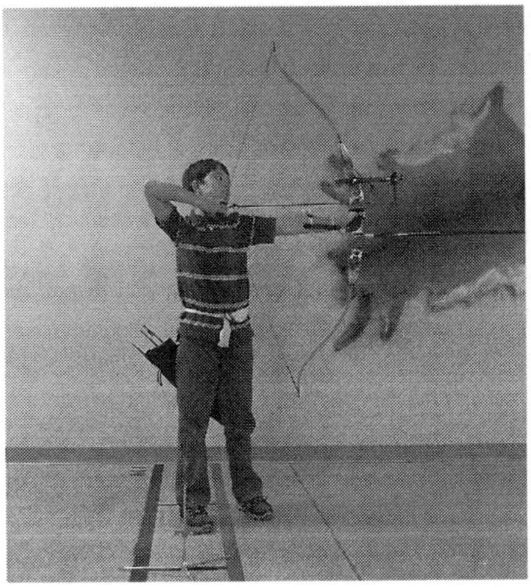

7. Aim

- Focus on the point you want to hit (if using sight)
- Focus on the point of aim (if not using sight)
- Relax while back gets tense

8. Release the String

- Let the string go
- Don't let go of the string
- Don't Relax (maintain tension in back)

1. Follow Through

- Hold form until the bow finishes its bow
- Relax

Communication

So much has been written about how we communicate that I do not want to belabor this subject more than is necessary. I am going to boil it down to just a few key concepts. If you can keep these in mind and adopt an attitude that "effective communication, while difficult, can be learned," you will do well. Here goes!

Basic Communication Principles

1. *Know Your Audience* Before you open your mouth, consider who you are talking to. If an eight-year old asks you why his arrows are always low on the target you might say, "Try holding your bow higher." To an elite archer the answer may be physical, technical, or even psychological and may take weeks or months to work out. You need to not only know your audience when considering how you communicate, you need to learn the signs that communication isn't happening. Fidgeting eight-year olds, teenagers with rolled eyes, or adults looking off into space are not clues that you have them enthralled. You've lost their attention.

2. *Be Congruent* What you say has to mesh with how you say it and with what you do. Have you ever asked a spouse or friend the question, "Are you still angry with me?" Can you tell whether or not they are still angry from the words of the answer, "No, I'm not still angry with you."? I can use those works with conciliation in my voice and you would believe I wasn't angry . . . or I could say them sarcastically and you would know I was still quite angry with you. There isn't a three-year old on the planet who can't tell when 'Mom has had enough' and it has nothing to do with the words Mom is using. How you say something turns out to be much more important than the words you use!

You not only have to link the words you use to how you say them but also to your actions. The old saw of "actions speak louder than words" is more than a little true. If you say one thing and do another, people—especially youths—will quickly adapt to the "real rules," the ones based on your actions, not your words.

3. *Keep it short, coach*! In my own coaching I have a problem of giving more information than was requested so I developed the habit of asking students, "Do you want the long answer or the short one?" The short answer is one or two sentences, never longer. The long answer . . . well, they asked.

It is worth repeating—if you can keep these in mind and adopt an attitude that effective communication, while difficult, can be learned, you will do well.

Bring In Other Coaches

Some coaches, myself included, get in over their heads. Do not be afraid to bring in other coaches. You can ask a coach you have a relationship with for advice over the phone. You can bring in another coach who is an expert on something you are weak on. None of these efforts, done occasionally, will undermine your role as coach. In fact, it will strengthen the relationship you have with your archers.

A few years ago Claudia created a JOAD competitive team for our local, promising teenaged archers. She asked two local coaches to take responsibility for the program and within just a couple of months, they had arranged for an USA Archery Level 4 coach to come out and do a three-day coaching seminar with the young archers. They passed the hat to acquire the coaches fees; one of the parents donated a roundtrip airfare coupon and the seminar was on! For three days, Bob Romero, fresh from coaching the U.S. Compound Men's Team at the FITA World Championships in New York, flew out and put on a fabulous seminar for the kids and their parents. Does this sound risky for a coaching relationship that was only a couple of month's old? The kids were all very grateful to Coach Romero but especially to the team coaches who made it all happen. That group is more cohesive than ever before because of the experience they all went through.

So, call in another coach to help when you need it. And respond to other coach-

Having a coach fresh from leading the Mens Compound team at the 2003 World Championships really gets an archer's attention! Here Bob videos one of the team members while Assitant Coach Steve Ross looks on.

Team members were taught how to give constructive feedback to one another.

Bob even had meetings with parents and other members of support teams on how to provide the support and structure young competitors need.

es who call with a need you can fill. You might end up being the star on the program!

The Five Ps Are Really Just One

The "Five Ps" are: Persistent Practice Prevents Poor Performance. These add up to one really big P—P as in Planning. This is something you really have to do—or you will end up being (or appearing to be) foolish. Since I have a great deal of experience in that area—appearing foolish!—let me explain why planning is necessary. I have to tell you a story first. My niece, a grammar school teacher, once asked me to come talk to her Grade 1-2 class. I agreed upon doing a half hour session. I worked up half an hour of material, then remembered stories of grammar school teachers talking about how fast things could go in the classroom, so I added another half an hour, and—for safeties sake—another half an hour of material. Guess how fast I went through that hour and a half of material. I didn't make it to the 20 minute mark before I ran out of stuff to say and show. Archery group lessons can go like that.

Planning ahead is paramount to coaching. If you run out of things to do a half hour into an hour and a half lesson, you are in trouble. Plan ahead. Have extra activities (balloons, novelty targets, instructive or inspiring archery videos, something) you can pull out at a moment's notice.

What Can I Do?

Things to Do

- If you have serious competitive archers, every time you get to talk to an accomplished archery coach, ask them if they do stints as "guest coach." If they do, ask about a few particulars (what they tend to do, what it would cost, etc.) and get their card. While it may sound like a lot of trouble and/or expense, you may be surprised at how many parents step up with assistance and money to make it happen.
- Make up a handout for the "Nine Steps" or other shot sequence to give to your archers to explain what a shot sequence is. The key element is that the sequence is used to break down a shot both physically and mentally. If a student finds herself thinking about her stance between steps 5 and 6, it is a clear sign something is wrong and it is time to start over.
- Keep a notebook of all of the exercises that can be used to "fix" a particular problem. Unlike golf, there aren't a zillion books on the market with drills to fix problems, so you'll have to make your own. (I know, I know; I'm working on it!)
- When you shoot, keep an account of your own practice habits.
- From time-to-time sit down and evaluate yourself on some of the things you would like to be doing as a coach. One system is to give yourself a score on a 0-10 scale (just like scoring an arrow), that way your total score gives you a measure of your opinion as to whether you are making progress as a coach and the

individual scores tell you how you are doing on each aspect.

Things to Read/View

Some of the general coaching resources (see the Resources segment at the end of the book) give some guidelines about how to run group/team practices. Unfortunately, they don't have much to say about working with individuals and individual sports.

A Model Curriculum

Both Claudia and I are big fans of the principle of not reinventing the wheel. It is not necessary for you to invent a curriculum for teaching archery classes or for having individual coaching/practice sessions. When you are teaching groups use one of the existing curricula. When teaching individuals, you should jointly make up a practice plan.

- USA Archery's JOAD Program (It stands for Junior Olympic Archery Development.) has a well-developed program for youths through the age of 18. There are stages your archers can work though, each of which has an award associated with it. USA Archery has been doing this for a lot of years!
- Check in with NADA (*www.teacharchery.org*). They have an excellent "Drills and Skills" booklet with exercises, instruction, and an evaluation program. The student booklets and accomplishment medals are quite reasonable.
- The Pasadena Roving Archers (Pasadena, CA) has an extensive program of archery courses for the public. One of their officers, Van Webster, wrote up the curriculum they use in an article for *Archery Focus* magazine ("Designing an Archery Course" by Van Webster, *Archery Focus*, Vol. 8, No 6, *www.archeryfocus.com*)

8

The Styles of Archery

Introduction

There are a great many different ways to shoot arrows from a bow. First, there are different kinds of bows: longbows, horse bows (Yes, really!), Japanese yumi, compound bows (one cam, two cam, cam and a half(?)), recurve bows, crossbows. Then there are quite a different number of techniques to be used in shooting any one of the kinds. For example, for just compound bow archers, the National Field Archery Association recognizes six shooting styles (see the graphic later in this chapter for details):

Freestyle
Freestyle Limited
Bowhunter
Bowhunter Freestyle
Bowhunter Freestyle Limited, and
Barebow

(and there are others for recurve and longbow archers) and this is just one association! Then there are the divisions (Youth (3-4 age groups), Adult, Seniors (2 age groups)) and gender (male-female). I have a friend who says that the solution to all of these complications is to reduce the number of competition categories to just two: left-handed and right-handed. He, of course, is left-handed.

Each of these shooting styles has its own set of rules in addition to the common rules all archers must follow in competition. It is because of competitions that all of these rules exist. Each rule, I am convinced, started with somebody (who was just outshot) pointing at another archer and saying, "He cheated!"

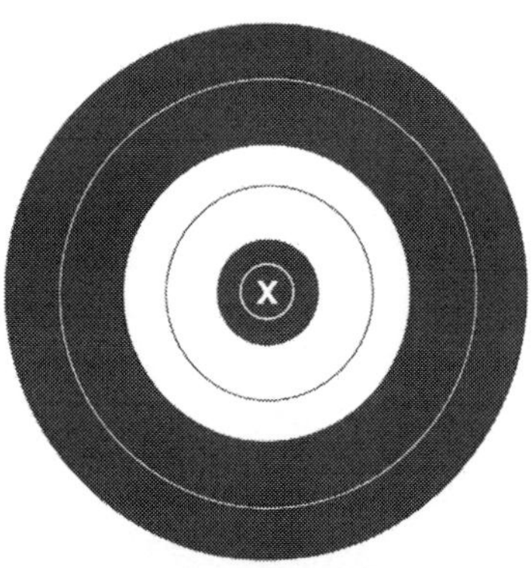

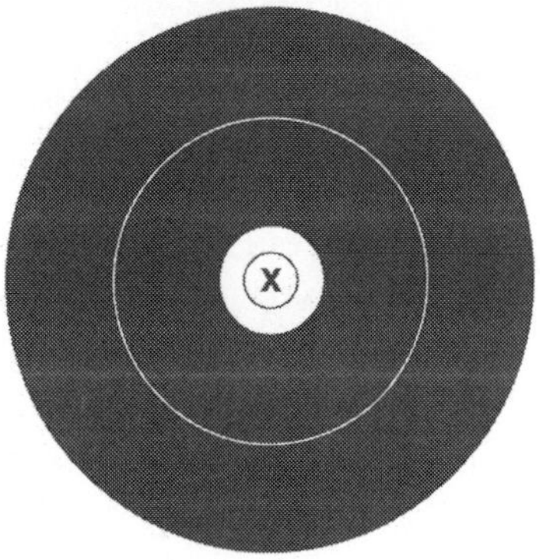

From top to bottom: an NFAA "Field" target, a life-like 3-D target used for hunting simulation games, an NFAA paper animal target (used similarly to 3-D targets but are much cheaper), and an NFAA "Hunter" target. Elsewhere in this book you will see many examples of the international FITA target used by both USA Archery and the NFAA.

Then there are differences in targets shot at. Most associations have created their own targets. In most cases, the distinction is not where to shoot (if the target is paper, try the middle) but in how to score it. USA Archery has targets with 10 scoring rings (worth 1-10 points, sensibly) while the NFAA has targets with five scoring rings (worth 3-5 points) but they somehow left off the rings worth one and two points. The 3-D crowd shoots simulated hunting scenarios with, this is where the "3-D" comes in, three dimensional targets (life-like lions and tigers and bears, Oh, my!). Some of these, like life-sized elephants and "Big Foot," have to be seen to be believed.

So, what must a coach know and be able to do with regard to coaching people who want to shoot a particular style?

What to Know About Styles

First, you do not need to go out and buy or steal all of the rule books available. FITA's and the ASA's rules are available online for free—also, they are deadly dull reading! So, a good place to start is to pick up some basic information about the styles that are shot in your area. If your local club is an NFAA affiliated club, start with their styles (*see the graphic for a thumbnail guide to NFAA styles*). If you are in a hotbed of Olympic-style archery, learn USA Archery's styles first. If 3-D archery is hot, check out the IBO and ASA rules. (See "Archery Alphabet Soup" at the end of the book for descriptions of these organizations and contact information.)

You are much better off initially knowing where to look things up than trying to memorize everything. And, I guarantee that you will get confused. In the NFAA, "Seniors" are so-designated as being older than ordinary adults (as in "senior citizen"), but in USA Archery, "Seniors" are so-designated as being older than "Juniors" who are 18 and younger. Both the NFAA and USA Archery have a youth division called "Cub" both with different age restrictions, of course. Sheesh, its enough to make your hair turn gray.

That graphic of the NFAA shooting styles (*see right*) is something I created because NFAA members were coming to NFAA-style events at our old club and not really knowing what style they shot . . . or what age group they were in, or . . . and guess who had to explain it to them? The same confusion confronts newer archers and coaches in all the other organizations.

This is something you need to know how to keep up with.

What to Know About Competitive Divisions

Not only does every archery association make up its own rules, but they are constantly tinkering with them.

This becomes important when students are involved in competitions (which, of course is really desirable). So, the key thing is to realize you are probably going to need to check with the organization to confirm the age, gender, and style categories. I can't tell you how many times I had to tell NFAA parents that their children did not shoot the same style as they did (because only four styles were/are allowed in the Youth Division), but it is a big number. Making assumptions about rules doesn't work (even for me).

Ask lots of questions. Identify people who seem to be experts on the rules, etc. and call them with questions. This is a long, slow process and "mistakes will be made," so keep your cool and work with event organizers to make your student's experience a positive one.

What to Know About Teaching the Various Styles

If you were to take someone who knew absolutely nothing about archery to a large archery competition, they would probably look at all of the different styles of archery and think they were all "doing the same thing, the same way." To some extent, they are right: Step 1—Put an arrow on the bow, pull it back, let it go. Step 2—Repeat.

Of course, the details are innumerable. Before you agree to teach someone a particular style of archery, you had best know the fine points.

When I was just getting started in archery I thought a "long bow" was something contrasted with a "short bow." I have since competed in USA Archery's Traditional National Championships in "Traditional Longbow" (and won a medal, too!). I also have had lessons in how to shoot an Olympic-style bow (although I am still somewhat pathetic with that beastie, as it is a style best taken up when young). I am still trying to find somebody to teach me crossbow.

The rule here is you can't teach what you don't know.

The good news is that the archery newbie was right, most archers are "doing the same thing, the same way." And, at the same time, even something as simple as "pulling back the bowstring" has nuances and fine points.

NFAA Shooting Styles

If You Shoot ... *and you are an ...*	Adult	Young Adult/ Youth/Cub/PeeWee
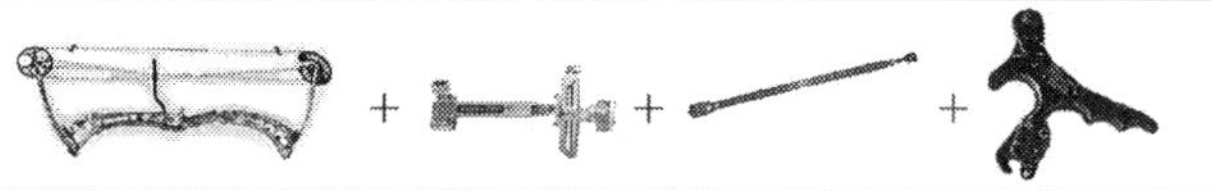	FS	FS
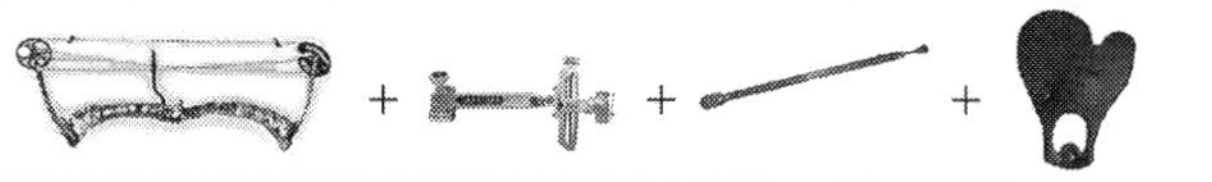	FSL	FSL
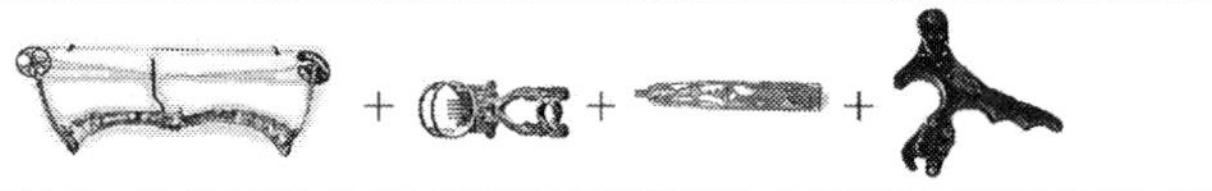	BHFS	FS
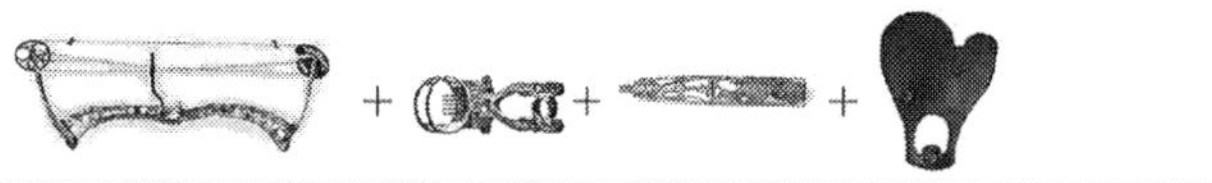	BHFSL	FSL
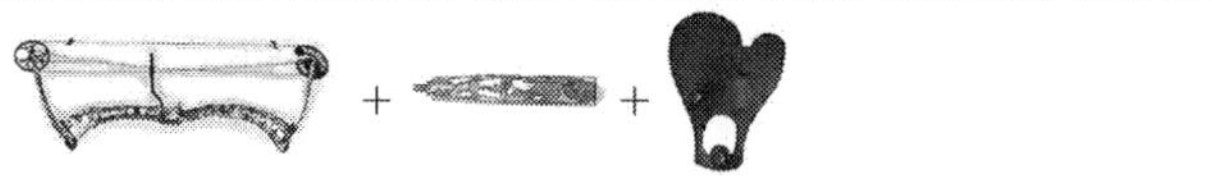	BH	BB
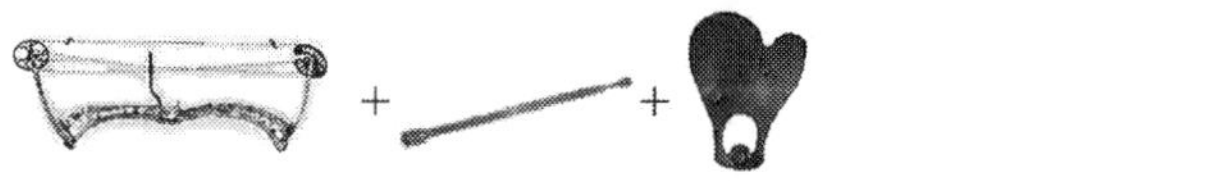	BB	BB
	Trad-RC	BB
	Trad-LB	BB
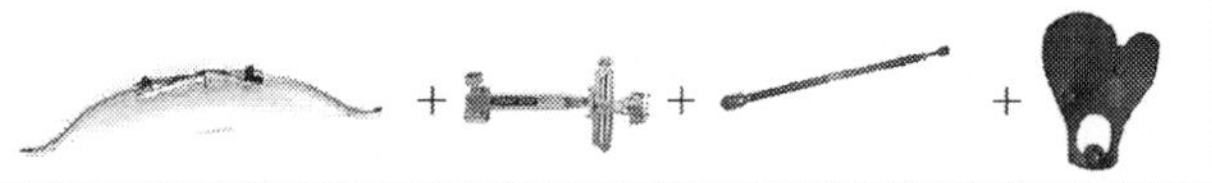	FSL-R/LB	FSL-R/LB

Key

FS = freestyle
FSL = freestyle limited
BH = bowhunter
BHFSL = bowhunter freestyle limited
BHFS = bowhunter freestyle
BB = barebow
Trad-RC = traditional recurve
Trad-LB = traditional longbow
FSL-R/L = freestyle limited–recurve longbow (basically FITA Freestyle)

Note—In the Junior Division—Young Adult (*15-17 years old*), Youth (*12-14 years old*), Cub (*under 12 years old*)—there are only four styles recognized—FS, FSL, BB, and FSL-R/LB.

My attitude I borrowed from Harvey Pennick, the famous golf coach, and is: "If you shoot arrows, you are my friend." Everyone I meet can teach me something and I am always looking for it. Everyone I meet in archery is either a student or a coach—the best coaches are both students and coaches.

National Championships

One of the great things about archery is that the competitions are open, that is, with the possible exception of the Olympic team trials, you can participate in virtually any competition by paying an entry fee. The NFAA and USAA even have an agreement by which members of either organization can compete in the other's national championships without being a member of the other organization. (Realize that most of these organizations have a "Guest Class" for persons not members of that organization. Giving out awards to non-members would be the demise of any archery organization.)

So, your students, after being in archery for six months, might end up in a large regional or state or even national championship. They might just ask for your help. Under those circumstances, your feet are being put to the fire and you are going to

USA Archery's Outdoor Target Championships (above) are shot on a flat lawn. The National Field Archery Outdoor Championships (next page) are typically contested in the woods and hills.

Field archery outdoors is a summertime activity, yet over the winter the National Field Archery Association and other archery organizations sponsor large indoor competitions.

have to call upon more established coaches. Elsewhere in this book I write about how it is really important to connect with other coaches upon whom you can rely when in situations like this. Just like in shooting archery, you are better off practicing with people better that you are.

What Can I Do?

Things to Do

- If your specialty is USA Archery styles, call up an officer in a local NFAA club to see if there is someone in the club willing to give you a primer on NFAA styles ... and *vice-versa*.
- Attend a competition of an organization you know little about. During the competition there are always folks who have little to do who will be more than willing to have somebody to talk to. Observe the practice area before and after competitions. Ask a lot of questions, but don't make a nuisance of yourself. You will learn a lot.
- The Texas Archery Association's website has a wealth of resources regarding Olympic-style archery (and JOAD programs, and building your own tools, and....) They have a one-page freebie that lists all of USA Archery's divisions and styles including the distances shot in competition! Check it out under "JOAD Resources" at *www.texasarchery.org* (look for "What Are Your Distances and Target Sizes? A Chart;" there is also a downloadable and printable PDF version).
- Consider, if you are not already a member, joining one of the archery organizations active in your area. While you will probably hear plenty of complaints about this or that (archers like to gripe like all patriotic Americans), consider what archery would be like without them. (Do you remember playground sports where arguing occurred more often than playing?) Also, almost all of the organizations require you to join an organization before you take a Level 2 Coach's certificate.

Things to Read/View

Here are some archery style resources you might be interested in. There are more in the back of the book. (📖 means "book" and 🎥 means "video")

📖 NFAA Constitution and Rules Should be free, but its not. (It is republished every year by the NFAA, *www.fieldarchery.org*.)

📖 FITA Rule Book The FITA Rule Book (used by USA Archery) and much more is available free at *www.archery.org*. Look under "Rules" and "Publications."

9

Got Style? An Exploration of Archery Coaches' Styles

Introduction

A fair amount has been written about coaching styles in the general coaching literature and even in the literature of archery. Claudia and I have trained quite a few archery coaches, mostly through the auspices of NADA, and the topic of coaching style always comes up. In the old NADA Level 2/Intermediate Instructor training three radically different coaching styles are examined. We will explore those descriptions below, but even in this case our recommendation is consistent—Just Say No! In other words, I believe that a coaching style is not a "garment you can put on or take off" is wrong-headed.

Some Coaching Styles

You only have to turn on a television set to see any number of coaching styles. A picture of a coach of a professional football or basketball team screaming at a referee is easily found. Hmmnn . . . coach as screaming motivator; I don't think that would work with archers who are supposed to be on the low end of the adrenaline spectrum. So, is this a coaching style? To scream or not to scream? Well, no. Let's look at the coaching styles that show up in so many places (USAA/NFAA training manuals, *Successful Coaching*, 2nd Ed., etc.).

Command Style This is exactly what it sounds like: you are a general, your student a soldier. His job is to take orders, yours is to give them. I played a lot of sports as a youth, from Little League to college basketball, and I can't remember coaches

doing anything but telling me what to do. Some did it in a loud voice, others more softly, but it always started out with "Here's what I want you to do. . . ."

Submissive Style In this style, you as coach allow almost anything to go. You know, "Gee, guys, I don't know if that is a good idea . . . well, if you want to, go ahead." This is a coach in over his head or trying to be friends or was born without a spine. I am not sure why this is a recognized coaching style as it is hard to identify that these people do any coaching.

Cooperative Style With a name like this you can be sure that this is the style that is expected to be most appealing. Cooperative coaches work with athletes and while they put "athletes first and winning second," they make their share of the decisions. They allow the athletes to make some of the decisions, though.

But Then . . .

But what about the myriad other coaching styles that are not mentioned? One physical education source I have lists the following styles:

- Command Style
- Practice Style
- Reciprocal task Style
- Self-check Style
- Inclusion Style
- Guided discovery Style
- Problem-solving Style
- Student-designed Style
- Student-initiated Style, and
- Self-teaching Style.

Whew! They called this set of coaching styles the "Command – Self-Teaching" continuum. They didn't go into the "Direct—Indirect" or "Formal – Informal" continua (for which I was grateful).

So, why are just these three styles (mentioned before) in the archery coach trainings? Is it possibly to "sell" you on the "cooperative" style which is certainly to be recommended for mature athletes, but. . . . This is a little bit like the spoof on dog food commercials that goes: "Look how much friskier the VitaCrunch dog is that the dead dog over here." The alternatives to what they are pushing aren't particularly appealing.

The other problem I have is where these folks take you after they describe these "styles" of coaching. Are you supposed to pick one of these styles and adopt it as your own? Are you supposed to realize that we all have a little of each of them in us? Is it just to start a discussion about how we are to coach athletes? They will talk about these, but they don't get around to saying why having "a style" is to your advantage.

But I will—Just Say No to Coaching Styles!

Let's Start Over

In my book, you have a style when Time magazine says you have one; otherwise you don't. Look, coaching archery isn't about style. Being an archery coach is being part of a relationship: the coach-athlete relationship. And, no, I am not going Dr. Phil on you. The coach-athlete relationship is simply the structure for what each of you wants to get out of interacting with one another.

Why does an archer-athlete ever want to talk to a coach? It is only because they want something. They want help. They want to be right (one coach can be played off against another). They want what another pair of eyes can give to them. They need tuning help. They want to learn how to shoot a bow like Legolas. Often as not, they signed up for a summer camp, recreation department, or 4-H, or JOAD program because it looked like fun and you are the coach they got. So, don't expect them to be perfectly clear about what they want. They may want to be a winner and they noticed some of your student-athletes winning, so maybe they should be coached by you, too. But, they want something out of the relationship, otherwise they wouldn't even be speaking to you. And, no, they are not just mercenary little boogers; they just want what they believe you have to offer.

So, why are you coaching? Are you in it for the money? Did you volunteer "for the kids?" Is your ego involved? Is it because your kids got involved in archery? I really don't want to get into this in any depth, but I encourage you to take a little time to identify what you want to get out of coaching archery. One of the things I have on my list is "It is fun!" If coaching an athlete ceases to be fun, I start asking myself why I am continuing to work with that athlete. This is just one of the reasons why you need to know *why* you are a coach.

With this view of things, it is very important for both of you to know what each of you wants from the relationship. This may not be readily observable. I had a very promising young compound archer consult me on why his groups had gone from round and small to very tall and narrow. I then told him there are many reasons why his groups might have spread out that way. Before I could begin questioning him on various form flaws, he shot another arrow and the right half of his rest fell off. "Maybe that was it," I said. And that was the end of that coaching interaction.

I highly recommend you find out what your athletes want and then either try to give it to them, talk them out of it, or pass them off to another coach. The discussion goes along the lines of the athlete telling you what they want and you telling them what you think you can do to help. If you agree to work together, you will only stay together as long as it is working for you both. The athlete is progressing to his/her goal and you are having fun (or whatever)—or—you are not, and it is time to consider moving on.

It's About Communication, Not Style

Make it a conversation. The best coaching is not a lecture. When you are offering your observations try to remember that you are just one observer, with all of your failings and biases. You are not endowed with perfect insight, knowledge, or skill.

> *"Start by asking questions. You need to seek information as well as to offer your own views. If you are going to offer advice as to how to perform a task, you need to be clear what the recipient was trying to do. It is often useful to ask a recipient what he thinks of his performance, and how it can be improved."*

I offer the quotation above not only because it is extremely good advice, but also because it came from a business book (*Getting It Done* by Roger Fisher and Alan Sharp, HarperBusiness, 1998). The secondary point is that you will be finding good coaching advice in all sorts of places. The primary point is that when someone is asking for coaching, they are asking for advice, but few people want someone telling them, "Oh, you are doing, this, this, and that all wrong!" Fischer and Sharp go on to say "Rather than thinking of observations as divided between positive and negative, they are more usefully divided into two categories: "What Worked Well" and "What to Do Differently." Thus instead of evaluating the performance ("That was great" or "That could use some work.") you can reinforce its strengths and develop concrete ways to improve it. Sounds like the "Oreo Technique," doesn't it. (If you don't know what the Oreo Technique is, it is merely to give suggestions for improvement sandwiched between two reinforcements of what worked well. It makes the suggestion for improvement ("What I would like to see on your next shot . . .") easier to hear and it guarantees that more than half of your comments will be perceived as being of a positive nature.)

This is not a style *per se*; I consider it to be merely good manners. The more your coaching sounds like a focused conversation, the better and more effective you will be. Listen for it.

> *"Communication consists of two parts—talking and listening. Of the two, listening is by far the more important."* (Roger Fisher)

A wise man, Roger Fisher.

Coaching Style is About How

Once you and your athlete have decided what you want, it is up to you to figure out how to get what you both want. When you get around to the "how" you are now in the realm of style. If your athlete is a mature adult, the Command Style may not work as well as if the athlete were eight years old. Adults don't like to be told what to do; children don't either for that matter, but they are more inclined to take directives. Children certainly don't want long-winded instructions, but adults usually want some connection made between the task and the outcome on the order of "if you do this, then the benefit will be that."

A classic theme in kung fu movies is a student seeking something (usually revenge—don't ask me why) who then finds a teacher and begs him to teach him. The teacher always refuses, of course, and the student has to beg and plead to be accepted as a student. Then the student is given a long series of manual tasks that seem to have nothing to do with kung fu (Wax on, wax off!) but which teach the skills the student sought. In the culture behind kung fu movies, all teachers have the command style and students, if they want to learn, must accept a subservient position. I don't think this is the way to go, but it is an option; it is *a* way to go. My college basketball coach told me, "Some of you need a pat on the back and others a kick in the pants. It is my job to figure out which."

The trick is that the same archer may need a kick in the pants one day and a pat on the back on another. If you are locked into a "style" you may not notice and keep kicking when you should be patting or vice versa.

One Thing at a Time

One way to always be "on task" is to identify those things an archer wants to work on then tackle them one at a time. My partner Claudia starts out all budding archers on the "one next thing" path. All of her archers can tell you the "one next thing" they are working on. People can really only concentrate on one thing at a time and, when working with coaches, archers should only be working on that one thing. This creates an easy measure of progress. If "one thing" leads to another "one next thing," progress is being made. If the same thing is being worked on for extended periods of time, progress is marginal at best.

Of course, what the "one next thing" is plays a major role here. If it is target panic, it could take weeks or months to work out because it requires reprogramming an archer's shot. If it is something less loaded, say grabbing the bow upon release, progress could be seen in minutes, hours or days rather than weeks. Still the "one next thing" approach provides a structure to coaching sessions. You may have to come up with multiple ways to work on your archer's one next thing, so she doesn't get bored, but then that is why you are getting the big bucks, no?

Student-led Coaching

Another structure to support your relationships with those you coach is to consider student-led coaching. This is especially useful when you are working with a more

Archer Evaluation Form

Name of Archer ______________________________

Name of Evaluator ______________________________

Type of Bow ❐ Recurve ❐ Compound ❐ Traditional

Style (freestyle, barebow, etc.) ______________________________

Date ______________ Years Shooting ______ Years Competing ______

OBSERVATIONS/NOTES (WHAT WORKS, WHAT NEEDS WORK)

____

Equipment ______________________________

____

Setup (draw length, draw weight, arrow spine, etc.) ______________________________

____

Form ______________________________

____

____

Execution ______________________________

____

____

Video Observations ______________________________

____

____

____

Recommendation for "One Next Thing" ______________________________

____

____

____

mature archer. Please note I said "more mature," not "older." Some younger archers are mature beyond their years and some older ones behave like babies. To follow this approach, you don't take orders, but you sit and listen to one another. You ask the student to make the decisions. It may be that he or she asks you to make some decisions, but that is the archer's decision to do so, not yours. In this mode, you ask questions instead of issuing directives. You give options from which the archer chooses. Of course, you don't agree to anything you think is really harmful to an archer's progress, but the student leads.

No Style is My Style

(Boy, I am starting to sound like Bruce Lee.) I espouse no style. I would like to think I can come up with whatever my student-archer needs but, realistically, that is probably impossible. I hope I know when to let up, when to challenge, when to throw an athlete on his own resources, when to get angry, or when to be sad. I just try to be what I need to be to help who I am coaching.

I am limited by my personality. I am who I am. (Now I sound like Popeye.) I can be irritating. I can be challenging. I can be fun to work with. I can't turn on and off who I am, so I try to stick close to what is natural for me. I try to be aware of what my strengths and weaknesses are. I try to learn all of the time, learn to minimize my weaknesses as a coach. But, I am still better on the technical side than on the organizational side. I can help you tune your bow but am not all that helpful getting you to plan a competitive season, for example. I know this and I work at getting better on the organizational end.

If you can be honest with yourself as to what you are good at and what you are not so good at, and you are willing to keep learning, you can become a very good coach. And the topic of style doesn't even have to come up.

Moving On

Before leaving this topic, I mentioned before that if you weren't getting what you wanted from a coach-athlete relationship, it may be time to "move on." Athletes need different things during the various stages of their athletic endeavors and often that means different people, too. If the relationship isn't as productive as either would like, the best case scenario is that you can part as friends or, if not, at least amicably. Dragging out a coaching relationship that is not productive is in no one's best interest. Take some time occasionally to sit down with your athletes and assess how things are going.

What Can I Do?

Things to Do

- Write down your coaching philosophy (basically what you do, how you do it, and why). You may find that giving copies of this to parents and prospective archer-students can foster good communication.

- Sit down and make up a list of your strengths and weaknesses as a coach. Do not make the mistake of just working on your weaknesses. Look at each of these and decide if there is one thing you could do to make it stronger (yes, both of them). If it is important to you, make goals for doing any of these and include your progress on those goals whenever you evaluate your coaching self.
- Make a list of what you want to get out of coaching (respect, sense of accomplishment, fun, etc.). Read this list every so often to see if you still agree with it and to check on whether you are getting from coaching what you wanted.
- Make up a "What Worked Well and What to Do Differently" evaluation sheet to use when evaluating an archer's form or performance.

Things to Read/View

📖 If you want to read up on coaching styles, etc. you might look into *Successful Coaching* by Rainer Martens. I didn't recommend this book in the resources section as it reads too much like a college textbook (which it is). I got my copy on Amazon.com, used, for $0.99 plus shipping.

10

Coaching at Tournaments

Introduction

This chapter is about coaching at tournaments. Coaching at tournaments is one of my weaknesses and, as such, I am trying to learn as much about it as I can. I can share a few pieces of wisdom I have acquired along the way.

Coaching at Tournaments

If you decide to accompany a student or a group of students to a tournament and agree to coach them, here are some things to consider. Now these are just my opinions, you don't have to agree with them! Then we will look at tournament logistics and your role in that and finally what you might want to teach regarding rules and etiquette. (Yes, etiquette!)

1. *If you are going to coach, don't compete.* If this is a tournament you wish to compete in, don't try to coach and shoot at the same time. It is hard enough to do either; trying to do both will detract from both and you won't do either well.

2. *Don't go without a goal.* I won't coach an athlete at a tournament who doesn't have a goal. The goal I recommend for a first tournament experience is "to have fun and learn a lot about tournament archery and myself." For a seasoned archer I do not like the goal "I am going to win!" as winning is not something anyone has control over. A reasonable goal is "to achieve a personal best score by focusing on having a strong and steady bow arm." That is something that can be accomplished without anyone else being involved.

My job as coach is to help my archer achieve that goal. Without such goals, it is too easy to "dabble." For example, your archer complains that he is consistently low on targets. He needs to figure out why. You can ask a lot of questions, check his equipment, etc. but archery is a "feel" (kinesthetic) sport and the archers themselves have to figure what is wrong. If the shots feel right but land wrong, it may just be equipment (...or not). I feel my job is to keep my archer(s) focused and on track and the "track" is the one leading to the goal. You need to be able to support your archer(s) with technical knowledge and so forth, but mostly you want to just "be there" for them.

3. *Fitness Comes in the Gym; Technique Comes from the Practice Line; Mental Skills are Emphasized at Tournaments* There is a time and place for everything. If you have an archer struggling through a tournament and they are struggling due to fatigue, the best thing you can do is to have them focus on something attainable (Having fun?) until you can talk to them about their archery fitness level *after* the tournament.

If you have an archer struggling through a tournament and they are struggling due to flawed equipment, the best thing you can do is to have them focus on something attainable (Having fun?) until you can talk to them about their equipment or setup *after* the tournament. Of course, if something is broken, you should fix it, but a repair is quite different from a bad setup or a bad tune.

If you have an archer struggling through a tournament and they are struggling due to flawed technique, the best thing you can do is to have them focus on something attainable (Having fun?) until you can talk to them about their form flaws *after* the tournament.

If you have an archer struggling through a tournament and they are struggling due to a lack of mental skill, the best thing you can do is to work with them on their focus and mental state *during* the tournament. Each arrow you shoot is practice (an audition, a performance) for the next arrow shot. When a tournament experience seems to be going south, a coach's job is to focus her archers back on their goals or onto whatever they can learn from the experience.

Tournament competition is the only place I have found where student-archers come to realize the value of mental skills training.

Logistics

Claudia and I have a few peculiarities regarding coaching at tournaments, possibly due to the fact that we focus on young people. One is that we expect our student-archers to arrange their own transportation. We just don't want to be responsible for a young person's health and well-being, those are their parent's responsibilities. Once we agree to drive a student archer to a tournament we are legally responsible for what happens to them until we get them back home. Possibly more important, we are responsible for what they might do. Most young people are responsible and grateful for anything you do for them, but there are some ... and I could tell you stories ... but I am not going to. Use your imagination.

We also acknowledge there is a long tradition of taking other people along to tournaments. We think this is wonderful; we just don't do it for students we are

FITA Shoot Checklist

Here is a checklist for items that you may find useful at an outdoor FITA target competitions.

- ❏ Sunscreen
- ❏ Lip Balm
- ❏ Band Aids, first aid tape
- ❏ Sunglasses (Decide if you can shoot wearing them or not)
- ❏ Bug Spray (important in Midwest!)
- ❏ Hydration fluids (water, diluted sports drink) and water bottle.
- ❏ Energy Bars (Cliff bars, Fruit, etc)
- ❏ Distraction Materials (Music + Headphones, Magazine, books)
- ❏ Money for Food, T-Shirt, phone call
- ❏ Umbrella (rain and shade)
- ❏ Portable Shade
- ❏ NAA Dress code clothing—shorts/pants/skorts/skirt (navy or white)
- ❏ Rain Gear (if slightest chance it is needed)
- ❏ Hat (Make sure you can shoot in it)
- ❏ Venue Directions, Shooting Schedule
- ❏ Folding Chair(s)
- ❏ Pencil, Black Marker (Sharpie)
- ❏ NAA Card (or other organization membership card(s))
- ❏ Bow (with all accessories incl. tab/release) and at least 10 Tournament Arrows (numbered and with archer's initials on the shaft).
- ❏ Sight Marks (for the distances you shoot)
- ❏ Backup Equipment (, backup bow (if available), bowstring, nocks, finger sling, tab/release, arm guard)
- ❏ Repair Tools (Super Glue, dental floss, serving material, lighter, string wax, bow square, Allen/hex wrench for every screw on bow, knife, wallboard screw to remove broken nocks)
- ❏ Backup Arrows (at least six, numbered with archer's initials on them)
- ❏ Optics (bino's, spotting scope + tripod)
- ❏ Arrow Lube (needed for Ethafoam targets)
- ❏ Arrow Puller
- ❏ Bow Stand
- ❏ Chest Protector (if needed)
- ❏ Arm Guard

Thanks to Steve Ross (Coach of Nevada County Gold Team) for letting me use his list as an example.

coaching.

Other than transportation, there is a long list of logistical things that need to be taken care of. Here is a list made up by our good friend Steve Ross for his archer-athletes (*see previous page*).

Giving a copy of this list to your student archers (to share with their parents if they are young) is a good idea.

Etiquette and Rules

There is some kind of etiquette at any tournament you attend, even the most rough and tumble traditional jamboree requires a certain etiquette of its participants. I am not talking about rules, here. I am talking about what you do and say while you participate. Let's talk about this.

Rules It is imperative for any archer you are coaching to know the rules in force at any tournament they attend. It is not enough to hand them a rule book. Most of the rules regarding shooting and pulling arrows should be learned at the practice targets. Scorekeeping can also be taught there. But formal tournament rules usually aren't taught. For example, in serious field tournaments you shoot with your competition, typically in groups of four. There are rules about which targets you shoot. (For example, Birdie/Bunnie targets are shot in vertical sets of four from top-to-bottom or bottom-to-top, except in international competition where they are in square blocks of four shot in a "Z" pattern!) There is a rule that every so many targets you switch which two archers shoot first and which two shoot last. You also change who shoots on the left and who shoots on the right in those twosomes. These kinds of rules exist to prevent unscrupulous competitors from taking unfair advantage.

Part of the problem is that some competitors ignore the rules. In order for the archers you coach to be comfortable competing, you have to put on your teacher hat and teach them these rules. Don't leave it up to their shooting partners to do this for you.

You also want to gently warn them about those "unscrupulous competitors." They are few and far between but it is not entirely unlikely they will encounter one of them. (Again, I could tell you stories. . . .)

Archery Etiquette Let me start what I want to say about etiquette with a couple of stories. The first involves an archer in her late forties attending the World Archery Festival/Las Vegas Shoot for the first time. She came loaded for bear and with a desire to win. Whether she did or not is not the story. The story is that she felt at odds with her competitors. She did not understand that in her style, very few women competed and the same women had been coming to this shoot for many, many years and had developed competitive friendships. They came to the Vegas Shoot not only to compete but also to socialize. Our newcomer was so focused on the competition that the cues to "join the party" weren't caught and the group felt she was being standoffish. The moral of the story, Grasshopper, is that archery is a social sport and you have to be aware of the climate when you jump in. It is not unreasonable to expect that the social aspects be confined to before and after the shoot or, at least, to the periods between ends or targets, but I have seen groups of archers well used to one another who continue to talk, even at full draw.

Our advice to newish competitors is to introduce yourself to your group and politely enquire as to whether the others know each other or have shot with each other a great deal. If either of those is the case, expect a different social climate than if your shooting partners are all strangers. Also, if you are part of the "in crowd," make a special effort to explain the situation and cut the newbies some slack.

The second story concerns a very promising nine-year old Olympic-style archer Claudia coached at her very first tournament (*see photo*). We did all of the usual preparation. A parent was along to supply transportation, food, etc. What we weren't prepared for was the level of trash talking that went on between 9-, 10-, and 11-year old girls at archery tournaments. Claudia's young archer lost her mental focus several times and got caught up in trying to "beat" the older girls. She got settled back down by some astute coaching on Claudia's part and ended up in third place. She also ended the day running and playing with her "new friends" after the tournament.

That was just the setup; there's more. We were so amazed by the spontaneous trash talking between these young JOAD archers that we commissioned a tongue-in-cheek article for *Archery Focus* magazine entitled "Trash Talking." Most of the feedback on the article was that it was one of the funniest things our readers had ever read in an archery magazine. One subscriber, though, cancelled his subscription because he thought we were advocating the practice of "trash talking" and that none of his JOAD student-archers would ever stoop so low as to participate in such an activity.

So, the moral of the second story is "things are different in different places." What was a tolerated behavior in California was not tolerated in a Midwestern state. So, some flexibility is needed. As with raising children or dogs, starting them out always on their best behavior allows for some relaxation of that behavior later on (if appropriate). Starting out "free and easy" may lead to hurt feelings or worse.

There is one thing we insist on from our archers and that is how to complement other archers. We advocate to our students that they never comment on any archer's performance other than possibly a nice group of arrows in the target. Even those comments can go awry in that your archer might say "Nice group!" based on what he sees, but that may be interpreted as sarcasm if the archer owning those arrows was used to shooting much tighter groups. In response to anyone saying "Nice group!" to any of our archers, we teach that the only correct response is "Thank you."

In the end, experience is the best teacher. Your job, as coach, is to just do a good job of preparing your charges to have a good experience to learn from.

Coaching No-Nos

There are some things you should never do at a tournament (and probably elsewhere, too). One of these is to comment negatively on people at a tournament. There is nothing good that can come from you making criticisms of archers or other coaches at an event. The comments invariably get back to those people and they, rightly or wrongly, resent the comments. Also, you should never offer advice to someone competing at a tournament. What could they possibly do, without some practice time, to incorporate what you have offered? More likely it will affect them negatively.

Once I was competing in the Pacific Coast Championships and had Frank Pearson, noted professional archer and coach, on my target. Toward the end of the competition he asked someone on the next target if he would like some advice *after* the tournament. The young man said yes and at the end of the tournament, Frank spent over a half an hour working with the archer as a coach, helping him immensely (I checked in with the guy afterward). That was well done. Offering free advice is one of the wonderful things about our sport. There is a time and place for it . . . but not *during* a competition, ever (which fact, of course, Frank knew and carefully acknowledged).

This brings up the point that your students are going to be receiving advice from many quarters. We have found it useful to train our students as to what to do when someone offers them free advice. We counsel them to respond, "Gee thanks, the next time I see my coach, I will tell him what you said." This simple sentence allows them to continue what they were doing without following the advice and not offending the advice-giver. It gives you, the coach, time to assess the advice. And between you and your archer, you can decide whether it is good advice or not. It really is our observation that young people who do not immediately take the advice of older and wiser heads, can get a reputation for being aloof (or worse). This simple practice works and keeps those older and wiser heads on the youngster's side.

Helping Them to Stand on Their Own

Our ultimate goal is always to help our archers stand on their own two feet. If we make them dependent on us, we may make a few extra pay checks, but we are not doing a good service. And it just isn't the case that archers want to, or can afford to, have their coaches on tap at every tournament.

One of the ways I try to stay true to this goal is to ask my charge "What is going on right now?" whenever I am inclined, or asked, to make an intervention. If they can figure out what is wrong on their own, they are one step closer to being independent.

What Can I Do?

Things to Do

- If you are "newish" to archery, make a date to attend an archery competition. Introduce yourself to people you encounter, explain your situation, and get ready to listen as archers, archery parents, and other archery coaches all offer you advice (good and bad, just like in everything else). Be prepared to take notes. You'll get to see what goes on at that kind of tournament. I have done this myself and then signed up to shoot in one to get the whole experience.
- Anytime you run into a very accomplished archer, pick her brains for advice regarding what you can do to help your charges at tournaments. Sometimes what coaches and archers think is helpful are at odds with one another. It pays to get many perspectives.
- Just as archers need a goal to attend a tournament, so do you. Make a few notes as to what you want to do/achieve and state them as goals, if you can. Keep this with you and review it from time to time at the tournament as it is easy to get swept up in what is going on and forget what it was you were trying to accomplish.

Things to Read/View

There hasn't been a whole lot written about coaching at archery tournaments. (I have been asking, but no takers, yet.)

Photo Courtesy of Lloyd Brown

11

Championship Level Coaching

Introduction

While this book is specifically directed to beginning-to-intermediate archery coaches, you may find yourself in the position of coaching at a championship level. How is this possible? Well, one of the very best things about the sport of archery is that everything short of the Olympic Team Trials is an open competition. This means that you can pay a small fee, show up, and compete at the local, state, regional, national, and even international levels and nobody will ask you for a qualification score.

Now, this could be like being thrown to the lions, but there are always more than a few other people who think that competing at that level sounds like fun, so it is a rare instance that anyone showing up is the worst archer on the field. This means that any archer participating in a major competition will find that they "belong" there, which is an enormous confidence booster. I freely admit that my first national championship competition was a little scary, that I felt I didn't belong in the illustrious group of archers, and that my goal for the tournament was simply, "Don't come in last . . . and have fun." What I found out was that I was far from the least proficient archer in my classification and that I belonged there. I also had a great time! I have since encountered any number of archers whose very *first* competition was at the state or national level. So, if a major competition comes to your neck of the woods and you think your students would benefit from the experience, by all means recommend it to them.

What also contributes greatly to this "level playing field" is that archers are grouped by style, age, and gender, so the people they compete against are much in the same situation as your students are.

Being a Championship Level Coach

So, one of your students takes the plunge and signs up for a championship competition and, whether you go (or not) or help them at the competition (or not), if they win, you are now the coach of an archery champion! You are a championship-level coach. So, what should you think of that?

This is something you have to decide.

I'll start my comments with a story. I had a student come to me asking for additional coaching. He was a member of a team and had a coach already, so I told him I would consult with his coach and if it was okay with him, it was okay with me. His coach told me the student would probably benefit from additional attention and had a list of three things the student needed to do that he had not yet done, and at the top of the list was getting properly spined arrows.

So, in working with the student, I helped him get properly spined arrows, his "one next thing" (see Chapter 7 on Practice), and then I moved out of the area, so we didn't work together any more. Within weeks the student competed in and took a state championship. Do I consider that student to be a student I coached to a championship level? My answer is "no," although some coaches count any student that they had *anything* to do with as a championship student whether they won that championship on their watch or not. I feel I didn't add anything to that student's performance that wasn't already in place.

Another student of mine, had started from scratch with me and had risen to a state championship (setting a new state record), so I now consider myself to be a championship-level coach. Now, I do not consider myself to be an elite coach, one who could work with archers at the highest level and contribute. I have just been focused so much on archers on the way up that I haven't worked with archers at that level . . . yet.

So, even though you've just been a coach for a short while, you may end up with champion archers under your guidance. It is a nice feeling, but I don't think you should evaluate yourself on how well your archers do at championship events. It is their sport; it is their accomplishment. What really counts is when they thank you for your contributions. They will tell you exactly what they got from you and when they do ... listen carefully.

Helping Your Students Prepare for Championships

Tournament preparation is covered in Chapter 9: Coaching at Tournaments, so is there anything special needed to prepare for championship tournaments? The answer is yes and no. For highly competitive archers there is a great deal of planning and preparation that goes into "peaking" for a particular championship, so for them the answer is very much "yes." For less experienced archers the answer is: yes and no. This is because there are so many kinds of archers.

One type of archer thrives on competition. This archer is energized and focused by the event. Her scores at competitions are higher than her practice scores. Does she need to do anything other than the usual tournament preparation? Generally not.

Another type of archer tenses up and performs worse in competition than she does in practice. She would benefit from some additional preparation.

The preparation here is almost entirely mental as all pressure is self-imposed. Claudia had a student attending her first competition who was so tense that she almost couldn't draw her bow. We were concerned she might pull a muscle. After she settled down, she went on to become a great performer (making the Jr. U.S. Archery Team). So, first experiences aren't necessarily telling. Also, experience is a great pressure reliever. Having been to a particular site or having competed in a particular event both function as pressure reducers.

A final thought on encouraging beginners to take a shot at a major tournament: make sure that they are fully prepared. Don't inflict a handicap on your student's competitors by sending a student in unprepared. One way to provide the necessary preparation (which is also fun) is to stage a mock tournament (with all of the rules, bells, and whistles) during a practice session. This was done for me and I found it very helpful.

So, How Does a Coach Help an Archer through that First (or Second) Pressure-packed Event?

The best thing is to make sure all tournament preparation is done. Then a couple of triggers are needed to help when the pressure is being felt. These must be practiced until learned so they will be remembered when needed.

The False Yawn One great tool to relieve pressure is a mighty yawn. One only yawns when one is sleepy or bored, so executing a yawn actually induces a little of those mental states. Try it, it will work for you, too.

Imagery of Practice Archery is a "feel" (kinesthetic) sport and to function well one has to be functioning subconsciously. And the subconscious mind cannot tell the difference between reality and something vividly imagined. The key here is for your archer to imagine shooting practice shots (all going into the center, of course) in a comfortable setting such as at the practice range or at home. The more vivid the imagining, the better! The ability to reproduce good shots requires the conscious mind to be engaged in something other than worrying about the score, worrying about the competition, worrying about the wind, etc. So, engaging the conscious mind in comparing the feel of the shots in the competition to the practice shots in the mind keeps all the worries . . . and the pressure they induce . . . at bay.

At a recent state-level competition, a cardinal rule was broken. (I won't mention the coach's name.) A young archer was coming off the line muttering, "I suck!" and other phrases not printable here. A coach walking by, in a spate of pity, suggested that this young fellow try to think back to what it felt like shooting a "bull's eye." Just to remember that because he knew how to shoot bull's eyes, he just need to remember. The coach walked away hoping the advice (that shouldn't have been given to a competing archer) would help. The young man came up to her a couple of ends later and shouted "It works!" and asked for and got a "high five." At the end of the shoot, the same ritual was repeated. Not commenting on the inappropriate coaching, it is a testament of how much the mind is a player in shooting arrows successfully.

During the competition, you can help your archer focus by reminding them of these tools and reassuring them that you have confidence in them. Your confidence can stimulate their confidence. Be warned, though, your doubts will also stimulate their doubts, so if you have doubts keep them to yourself. It is amazing how a comment you make to a coach at the other end of the field gets back to your archer faster than you can walk back!

After the Competition

After the competition, you may have an elated archer or a depressed archer. Neither will probably be receptive to any teaching at that moment. Celebrate or commiserate, whichever is appropriate and some time later, hours or days, be sure to have them figure out what was learned from the experience. I usually ask students to write down what they learned and a short list of what they will do differently next time, in other words—what worked well and what to do differently. Reading their own words from the last competition before they impart preparing for the next can make for powerful practices and powerful performances. At the very least it avoids making the same mistake over and over.

Advice to Beginning Coaches from Elite Coaches on Getting There

I have asked a number of elite coaches for advice to those of you who, energized by coaching, want to move up to the next level. These are people who have helped train me as a coach and who have established outstanding records as coaches themselves.

I asked for a couple of sentences to a short paragraph (or more) of their coaching wisdom. You can see in reading these that no matter how long they have been in the game, their passion is undiminished.

A Note to Beginning Archery Coaches from Larry Wise

You'll encounter many different types of archery students and I won't bore you with an analysis of those here. What is important to remember, I think, is that you can't motivate any of them; they have to motivate themselves as motivation always comes from within. What you can do is to get them excited about archery, their place in it, and how to take the next step.

If they see you as excited about archery, in general, and about their archery, in particular, they will have a better chance to catch what you are displaying. So first of all, you've got to be excited. I know that during my thirty-five years of teaching high school math it was difficult to call up any extra energy for my last class of the day but they deserved it as much as the others no matter what their level of talent, interest or behavior – ya just gotta do it!

In addition to being excited, you've got to be positive and caring. I always got better results from my students when I showed them that I cared about them and their interests. And when my thoughts, words, and actions were positive they always found it easier to work harder and smarter.

I had many good teachers during my school years so it was natural that I tried to be like them when I got my own classroom. The problem with that, I discovered, was that I was not "them" and what worked for them did not always work for me. So, when I learned to be myself, my teaching got much better, I enjoyed it more, my students enjoyed it more and it was more effective. My coaching is the same; it's better when I am myself, so you owe it to your students to be yourself.

In my quiver I carry an old faded arrow, an 1816, Easton XX75, Autumn Orange shaft that was part of the first dozen arrows I bought when I started competing again in archery. I think it was in 1976. I've carried it ever since then to remind me where I came from in this sport. I wasn't very good then—couldn't hit my butt with either hand shooting fingers—but I persisted, found my game with a Stanislowski release aid, and made an impact in professional archery over the years. That arrow in my quiver acts as my "peep sight" when I am sighting through the present trying to hit a target in the future. Without that rear sight in my mind I would never see how far I've come ... and never appreciate it! Be sure to remind your students—and yourself—about their starting point so they can appreciate how far they've come, where they are, and how far they can still go.

Keep well, shoot straight.

Larry Wise is possibly the most successful archery author in the U.S. As a professional archer he won the 1986 World Field Archery Championship in Scotland and is a five-time world team champion with many professional wins. He has been involved with USA Archery's Coaches Development Committee since 1996 and has taught in Level 3 & 4 coaching courses at both the Lake Placid and Chula Vista Olympic Training Centers. He still coaches privately and conducts one- and two-day shooting schools at clubs and archery shops. He coaches both finger release and mechanical release styles of shooting but his specialty is the mechanical release style.

Notes for Beginning Archery Coaches From Don Rabska

There are many documents available on how to be a better coach. Many do's and don'ts and sound rules to follow. At the top level, one of the best ways to improve your coaching ability is to study archers. Watch and listen intently and focus on your students. You will generally learn as much from them as they learn from you. If they ask a question and you don't know the answer, don't make one up, but don't rest until you find the answer. Building trust and confidence between student and coach is of paramount importance to a successful relationship. You can learn a great deal about a student by simply watching the way they draw their bow. Pay attention to your environment, otherwise how can you help them better understand wind shooting or how best to handle the effects of heat or cold. You will learn a lot from your students if you take the time to observe and listen.

I always believe that it is important to know "why". If a student asks why when you want to change some part of their form, you should know the answer inside and out. I never like the answer "because I said so." It commonly undermines confidence in the student and rarely helps foster a sound relationship.

Study shot biomechanics so you can help students improve form, and do this well in advance of mid to major events. You should always know the reason why something works and does not work. Archery is not Voo Doo, it is a sound mechanical principle based in the physics of mechanical application. Variables are too numerous to count and therefore, using solid mechanics can help eliminate or greatly reduce many of those variables. Knowing and understanding this scientific based concept with the ability to teach it, makes it far easier for the student to hit the center of the target with greater repetition.

Learn what motivates each and every student. They are all individuals and all need a slightly or significantly different approach.

Learn to work with every level of archer and every age group. Working with beginners to elite and from 8 to 80 years, gives you a far better understanding of how to best help everyone enjoy our wonderful sport.

Learn to be enthusiastic and helpful and not full of "don'ts." Be firm but fair. Be understanding and honest. Sometimes students need a sympathetic ear; sometimes they need a strong dose of reality.

Learn how to instill confidence. Athletes can lose confidence at the drop of a hat. Learn how to bring students back from doom and gloom to confident and courageous. There is no place for "careful" in archery. Teach them how to stomp "doubt" into kitty litter. Doubt is the little demon that chips away at the very foundation of confidence and hinders good performance. If an archer is truly confident, it makes little difference how "perfect" their form is. They can still shoot arrows in the center of the target with ample consistency.

Excellent technique will of course improve the ability to be consistent and clearly helps when it comes to major pressure. When an archer cannot feel their legs in a major competition is when they can rely on solid technique to get them through. This is why good technique, developed through the use of bone alignment rather than muscularity is important. Bones don't fatigue, allowing technique to remain virtually unchanged. Muscles fatigue, a fatigued muscle will recruit other muscles to help out. When this happens, technique changes and performance suffers.

Learn technique inside and out. Have the ability to judge someone's technique and work on each component, one at a time. Always start with the most critical and important part of the shot platform, then work on refining parts of lesser importance. If an archer has their shoulder in their ear and their draw elbow sticking out ninety degrees to the draw shoulder, you don't start off working on draw finger position.

Always be a student of archery. There is so much to learn that no one can know it all. Just enjoy the ride and try to learn something new about the sport each and every day. Archery can be a long and enjoyable journey with no discernible destination in sight. Have fun with it. Archery is a paradox in that is extremely easy and exceptionally difficult.

Study people and study your students. Learning their personalities in all situations will allow you to better help them succeed.

Learn how to say the same thing as many different ways as you can possibly think of. One of the suggestions might just evoke the right picture that will turn on the light bulb. Remember, it is not the words that come out of our mouth that constitutes communication, but rather the picture you generate in their head that truly provides clear and concise understanding of the message.

Also remember that there is no wrong way to shoot, there are simply better ways. The better way is the use of sound biomechanics that will allow your students to perform the same shot regardless of the number of arrows they need to shoot or the effect of environmental influences. Sound biomechanics naturally involves the use of ridged structural alignment, or bone alignment. The body is simply a system of joints and levers. If those levers are used naturally and efficiently, then muscle activity is reduced to a minimum and force vector alignment is constant. Constant and precise alignment, with consistent energy output through common lines of force, will produce maximum consistency with low effort.

An important rule to remember and to instill in your students is that the greatest amount of physical effort during competition is sure to produce the lowest scores. Good shooting comes from relaxed, fluid motion, precise timing and very little work.

Don Rabska is the Director of the Easton Sports Development Foundation which is devoted entirely to the development of archery, as they put it "The Easton Sports Development Foundation is an operating foundation established by international archery experts for the purpose of training and developing a pool of world class archers and other athletes able to compete at the highest levels. The strategy used to accomplish the Foundation's purpose is the creation of programs that develop archers at many levels in order to strengthen and deepen the available talent pool."

A Note to Beginning Archery Coaches from Bob Romero

Moving up in the coaching ranks will require as much effort, determination, and dedication as that required of the archer wanting to become a top level athlete. You will have to study, attend competitions, and work with as many archers as possible. Like most things, exposure is the key. The more experience you acquire related to technique, equipment, competition, and just being around the sport, the more you will benefit. Work with archers possessing a variety of skill levels if you can and try to work with both compound and recurve archers. Keep up with the latest techniques and by all means ask questions of the more advanced coaches. You will be amazed how much we are willing to share with an enthusiastic coach.

Bob Romero has been involved with high-level Archery Training for many years. He has coached all levels of archers from beginners to top-level Olympic recurve and compound archers, both in the U.S. and other countries around the World. Bob has coached U.S. World Championship Teams and participated, as a coach, in all types of camps at the Olympic Training Center in Chula Vista, California. He holds coaches seminars in many foreign countries and stays abreast of the most current archery techniques. Using computer analysis software he is able to diagnose and correct many problems that archers acquire along the way.

What Can I Do?

Things to Do

- When you attend tournaments introduce yourself to other coaches (during slack times) and see what you can pick up. Just hanging around with accomplished coaches, I have picked up many a good piece of information. Also, watch them work. You can learn a lot by just watching.
- Have your students keep a log book to keep their notes in. A small one which fits in their quiver works well. I have even gone so far as to give them such "notebooks." Ask your students to write things down that they learned that they do well and what they would change the next time they go to a tournament. Ask them to write on what is different between practice and competition and what could be done to make practice more like competition.
- Make it a practice to inform your student-archers about coming competitions. Often these have fliers that are downloadable off the Internet. Print copies to use as handouts as young people will need to take something home to talk to their parents about.

12

The 13 Commandments of Coaching Archery

Introduction

It is hard to remember everything you have read in this book, so I have tried to capture some of the essential points and frame them into easily remembered aphorisms. Here are 13 key points that are worth remembering.

1. The Joys Of Coaching – Find Them or Go Play Golf!

Master Coach Bernie Pellerite tells his students, "If you aren't having fun, you are probably doing it wrong." I think this applies to coaching as well. If you aren't having fun, you are going to consider doing something else. So, if you want to be there "for the kids," "for the program," or whatever, find the pleasure in doing what you are doing. Otherwise, you won't last.

2. Take It Seriously (You Gotta Wanna – Be Organized)

You may have started as a parent-volunteer or as a teen-aged archer helping out with the young kids, but if you want to be a coach, take it seriously. Plan. Be prepared. Make lists of things to do to make the program or your lessons better. Ask parents and athletes for feedback—be systematic, use a questionnaire so they can take it home, be thoughtful, and give you good feedback.

Make a list of your strengths and weaknesses. If your weaknesses are glaring, make plans to improve in those areas. Set goals for yourself.

If you want to be a better coach, "you gotta wanna," which means you have to want to enough to work at it.

And, please, I am not trying to turn coaching archery into a job. I enjoy learning about archery. So open yourself up to learning about those things that will make you a better coach, that's all.

3. It's Okay to Just Have Fun

Once I took a number of already (slightly) bent arrows and a group of kids to the 80-yard target on our field range and let them have a fling. I was going to have to straighten those arrows anyway, so it didn't matter that they were going to hit the ground again. Realistically, for those kids, it was about a par three. And it gave them practice in following the flight of others' arrows for retrieval later.

On another occasion I was assisting with an adaptive P.E. archery class at the college I was working at. We had a large field available and very lightweight bows, so I talked the professor into a flight shoot. We even had a competition for the longest shot with a prize for the winner (a quarter). On both of those occasions the sheer joy and exuberance of the archers is something I will always remember. They had a blast!

Sometimes, grinding away on planned lessons isn't the best thing you can do. Sometimes just having fun is a better alternative. This applies to beginners all the way up to Olympic hopefuls.

4. Style Doesn't Matter ("If you shoot arrows, you are my friend.")

My apologies to Harvey Pennick for the parenthetical statement. Harry Pennick was one of golf's greatest coaches and one of his books (worth reading, by the way) was titled "If You Play Golf, You Are My Friend," which was one of his aphorisms. The

point he was making was there was plenty of room in golf for all kinds of people, of all skill levels, of all backgrounds and stations in life.

I think this applies equally well to archery and its various "styles." I have learned different styles of archery (compound, recurve, longbow, crossbow, freestyle, barebow, etc.) because a number of students expressed an interest in it. We welcome all of the styles to lessons.

It doesn't matter what style someone chooses, if they shoot arrows, they are archers.

5. Get Out of Your Own Way

I do not mean to be rude, but the biggest impediment to your improvement as an archery coach is . . . you. This is true for me as well as for you (probably more so). Whenever your ego gets involved, you are definitely not making progress. If you hear yourself say, "I . . . (whatever)" often, you are in danger.

To be a good coach you have to focus on your students. You have to be yourself, but do not let *you* get in your way.

6. Praise Effort, Not Outcome

The outcome of an archery effort, a score or a place in a competition, is something that can be very exciting for your students. Hey, I still feel it myself! A good coach doesn't praise the outcome, but the effort. If you can congratulate that achievement while connecting it with what caused that achievement, you will be praising your archer and making a connection in his little pea-brain between the outcome (over which he has no control) and the effort made in practice or the competition (over which he has control).

As in the MasterCard commercials, the praise is valuable, but the connection, the learning of how that archer achieved what he did, is priceless!

7. All Archers Believe in Magic

This goes for archer's parents, too. All archers believe that equipment changes will produce magical results. These new arrows, that new bow, whatever, will produce that breakthrough score. Unfortunately, this is true for beginning archers who have less than well-matched equipment. If you replace bent arrows with straight arrows, scores go up. If you replace a poorly-fit bow with a well-fit bow, scores go up. But once an archer has equipment fit to him or her, the magic disappears.

I can't tell you how many times I have had archers asking about this or that new piece of equipment when they hadn't mastered what they have—or parents asking, "Wouldn't little Billy shoot better with a one-cam bow?" etc. The answer is almost invariably "no." Our culture has come to acquaint parental affection with how much money gets spent on our children. But once an archer gets set up adequately, equipment changes to accommodate growth are fine, but changing equipment in pursuit of a better score needs to be looked at skeptically. Practice is the gateway to performance, not equipment.

8. Performance is Determined by Self Image (Lanny Bassham)

I can't tell you how many young archers I see coming off the line after disappointing ends scowling (or swearing) and they often refer to themselves in the most disparaging terms. It is fairly clear that performance in anything is strongly linked to one's confidence in the task, in one's self-image. You must learn all you can about self-image and learn how to help your archer-athletes create healthy and productive self images. Be aware that this does spill over into the rest of their lives.

9. Paranoia Is Appropriate (Safety, Safety, Safety)

Being paranoid about safety is appropriate for archery coaches. If you are not convinced of this, go back and read the chapter on safety over again (and again, if necessary).

10. Never be Negative, Always Be Positive

Being positive does not mean being Pollyanna-ish. It means looking at the glass as if it were half full and not half empty. Both are correct descriptions but the positive description fosters better performance and attitude.

A Little League performer on his way the plate in a critical situation should never be told "Don't strike out." He might not have been thinking about striking out, but now that you have mentioned it, he begins to worry about that and the end result is unlikely to be good. If you give the instruction "Get a hit!" it is far more likely that will happen as that is what you want him to do.

Never tell an athlete what they are doing wrong, tell them how to do it right. That is being positive. Being positive affects how you are perceived by your archer-athletes, too. Positive coaches are generally liked more than negative coaches. (Okay, I know you noticed I used a negative "Never tell an athlete—", but I used it for emphasis and . . . I got your attention, didn't I?)

11. Get Connected / Stay Connected

While archery is an individual sport, coaching is never that. Seek help and advice from other coaches. If you strike up an acquaintance with someone you consider to be a very good coach, ask them if you can call or email them when you have questions. They will generally say "yes" and then your job is too not abuse the privilege.

If you develop a circle of coaches who can ask questions and offer advice freely, your job is going to be a lot easier. With modern technology you can send another coach a video clip of your problem archer and ask for help. There are all kinds of ways coaches can help one another.

It is generally true that you will "get" as well as you "give," so always be generous offering help to other coaches and it will come back to you.

12. Don't Reinvent the Wheel

An old saying is that "there is nothing new under the sun," and it is true in archery, also. If you have a problem, I can guarantee that others have had it before you. Try not to "reinvent the wheel" by creating a new cure for target panic, for example. There are already dozens of procedures that have track records. These are generally superior to anything you can come up with on the fly.

This is another reason to "always keep learning;" everything you can learn about coaching archers will come up and you will be prepared to deal with it.

13. Want What They Want

Archery is an individual sport. Your athletes are in it for reasons of their own. If not, and they are doing it because their parents want them to, or their big sister was an archer, or their father was a national champion, they are highly unlikely to succeed and be happy. To be a successful archer, your student needs to know why they are doing it and what their goals are. He needs to be in charge and, at the same time, he needs help from you. By careful listening and flat out asking, you can find out what they want and then your job is to help them. Eventually it is all about them. If you do not feel you can help them with "what they want" talk to them about it. Sometimes "what they want" changes and sometimes you need to suggest one of your archers need seek another coach.

A Final Note

I sincerely hope you have had as much fun working through this book as I have had in writing it. I also hope you got a lot out of the experience!

Happy coaching!

What Can I Do?

Things to Do

- Grab your bow and go shoot some arrows. Don't let coaching take away the fun of just shooting arrows!

End Matters

Archery Organization Acronyms (Archery Alphabet Soup)

Most of archery organizations/programs go by their initials, so I have listed them here that way.

ASA The Archery Shooters Association (*www.asaarchery.com*) An organization of professional archers. Sponsors (unmarked) 3-D tournaments in the U.S.

ATA The Archery Trade Association (*www.archerytrade.org*) Used to be AMO (Archery Merchants and Manufacturers Association). An independent body claiming to represent archery manufacturers, wholesalers, and retailers. Puts on a massive trade show every January.

FITA The International Archery Federation (Federation Internationale a Tir a l'Arc in French (hence FITA), *www.archery.org*) Governs Olympic-style archery internationally. Sponsors target archery competitions under Olympics and as world and continental championships for both compound (non-Olympic) and recurve. Has two official languages: French and English.

IBO The International Bowhunters Organization (*www.ibo.net*) Sponsors mostly (unmarked) 3-D competitions in the eastern U.S.

IFAA The International Field Archery Association (*www.ifaa-archery.org*) Governs field archery internationally. Overlaps with FITA as FITA has a field division. Sponsors target and field archery competitions indoors and out as world and continental championships.

JOAD The Junior Olympic Archery Development Program (*www.usaarchery joad.org*) USA Archery's youth program. In my opinion, one of the few archery-only youth programs that is completely developed.

NAA The National Archery Association aka USA Archery (*www.usarchery.org*) Governs Olympic-style archery in U.S. NGB (national governing body) for FITA; also has compound archers who compete up to the FITA world championships, but not in the Olympics. Sponsors target and field archery competitions indoors and out. See USAA.

NADA The National Alliance for the Development of Archery (*www.teach archery.org*, 352.472.2388) NADA was created to foster the growth of archery in the U.S. and is rapidly becoming the U.S. archery coach's association. Coordinates the training of Level 1 and 2 coaches for the NAA and NFAA as well as for NASP, the Air Force, and other entities. Provides liability insurance coverage for its members, making NADA membership the greatest bargain in all of archery.

NASP The National Archery in the Schools Program (*www.nasparchery.com*) A U.S. organization begun in Kentucky and promulgated through state fish and game departments to sponsor short-term archery in PE classes in grammar and high schools. Now in 40+ states and growing.

NFAA The National Field Archery Association (*www.fieldarchery.org*) Governs field archery in U.S. NGB (national governing body) for IFAA. Sponsors target, 3-D, and field archery competitions indoors and out.

USAA USA Archery, *www.usarchery.org*) Formerly just the name of that part of the NAA that was the National Governing Body (NGB) or official representative of the U.S. to FITA. Recently the NAA has adopted this as the name of the entire organization.

Books, Videos, Etc. for Further Learning

You won't find too many of these in your local library but it is still worth a try (especially since you can search the stacks of most public libraries online now), or ask your local bookstore to order them for you, or check out Amazon.com. Books have this icon (📖) while videos are identified with this one (🎥).

Freebies

There are a great many archery resources available online. Here are but a few:

- Easton Archery Spine Chart (available online from Easton Archery Products, *www.eastonarchery.com*, look under "Company" then "Downloads")
- Easton Arrow Tuning Manual (this was once available online free from Easton Archery Products and may still be (www.eastonarchery.com, look under "Company" then "Downloads" or do a web search for "Easton Arrow Tuning Guide" and it is probably available in multiple places) and was available in print form for a nominal charge)
- FITA Rule Book The FITA Rule Book (used by USA Archery) and much more is available at *www.archery.org*. Look under "Rules" and "Publications."
- Olympic Coach This free online magazine including back issues (Yes, it is for elite coaches, but its free!) can be had at *www.usolympicteam.com/12688.htm*.

- *Recurve Archer's Guide* (available online for free, Google it)
- *Discover Archery* (This isn't for you; it's for your younger students.) This is a free online magazine available at *www.afterschoolarchery.org*. Target audience is 11-12 year-olds; check it out!

General Coaching Resources

- *With Winning in Mind* by Lanny Bassham
  (available at www.lannybassham.com) This is an absolute "must have" for any archery (or other) coach who wants to understand the mental game. Over 100,000 copies sold!
- *Coach's Little Book of Wisdom* by Ron Quinn
  This very little book is very big on coaching kids—highly recommended if you intend to work with kids!
- *Coaching Kids for Dummies* by Rick Wolfe
  This book, like all general youth coaching resources is focused on team sports, and like all of the other "... For Dummies" series is very worthwhile.
- *The Parent's Guide to Coaching Physically Challenged Children* by Richard Zulewski While very general it does have a short bit on archery.
- *Your First Coaching Book* by The National Alliance for Youth Sports
  This tiny book, written mostly about team sports, has some good information in it for all coaches.
- *Coaches Guide to Sport Psychology* A Publication for the American Coaching Effectiveness Program by Rainer Martens, Ph.D.

Archery (Just Coaching) Resources

- *Peak Performance Archery* by Al Henderson
  This is it, the only archery coaching book published in the last fifty years and by master coach Al Henderson. This book is long out of print, but if you can find a copy read it, then read it again! (I just checked and Amazon.com had 10 used copies available.)
- *NFAA Constitution and Rules* Should be free, but its not. (republished every year by the NFAA, www.fieldarchery.org)

General Archery Resources

- *Fundamentals of Recurve Target Archery* by Ruth Rowe
  Great resource for recurve target coaches on how to start students on a good path (available from www.qproductsarchery.com)
- *Field Archery, A Complete Guide* by Michael Hamlett-Wood
  The writer is British so the focus is on their practices and rules, which aren't so different from anyone else's.
- *Traditional Archery* by Sam Fadala
  A good start if you, like me, started out knowing very little about traditional archery, U.S. style (available from Stackpole Books, 800.READ-NOW).
- *Complete Bowhunting* by Glenn Helgeland
  This is still available on Amazon.com (as a used book) and seems to be a solid resource on bowhunting. (I am not a bowhunter.)

Archery Fundamentals by Doug Engh
A good basic introduction to archery (available at most bookstores).

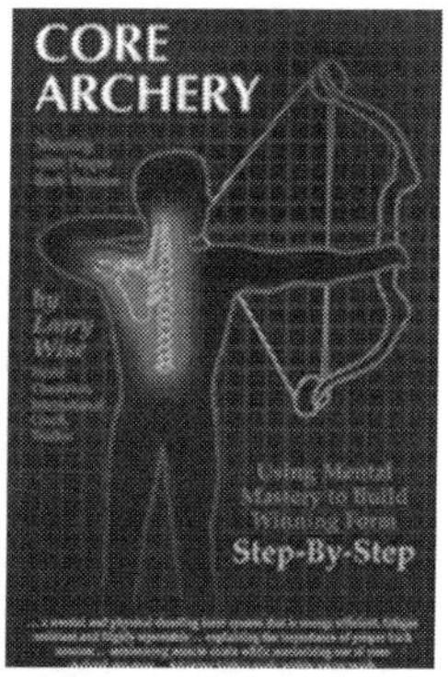

More Advanced Technique Resources

The Simple Art of Winning by Rick McKinney
Possibly the best selling book of its kind, it has become the bible of Olympic-style archery.

Archery Anatomy by Ray Axford
The most easily digested book on the use of bones and muscles in shooting a bow.

The Heretic Archer by Vittorio and Michele Frangilli
This book combined with McKinney's and Lee/deBondt's constitute a complete library on Olympic-style archery.

Understanding Winning Archery by Al Henderson
Al Henderson only wrote two books. This is by far the more famous and is still available (from Target Communications, *www.deerinfo.com*).

Core Archery, by Larry Wise
Larry Wise's last word on shooting a compound bow. The culmination of years of study, experimentation, and thought. Highly recommended (available from Target Communications, *www.deerinfo.com*)!

Handbook of Modern Recurve Tuning—Start to Finish by Richard Cockrell
While a little rough around the edges, you would be hard pressed to find a more comprehensive guide to tuning recurve bows. You would be hard pressed to find a more comprehensive guide to tuning recurve bows. The only ones I know selling it is USA Archery (www.usarchery.org) and Lancaster Archery (*www.lancasterarchery.com*).

Idiot Proof Archery by Bernie Pellerite
An omnibus on everything compound (available from www.robinhoodvideos.com).

Precision Archery, by Steve Ruis and Claudia Stevenson
Okay, yeah, it is my book but it is still really good—for intermediate to advanced archers.

Professional Archery Technique by Kirk Etheridge
This was the first book to describe the framing techniques then being used illegally in unmarked distance competitions. Addresses compound bows only (available at many bookstores)

Straight Talk from the Pros (by Carter Enterprises)
Not only for the release aid advice but advice along the way on shooting form and winning from top compound archers, this is a must view video. (available from *www.carterenterprises.com*)

- *44 Form Flaws* (by Bernie Pellerite)
  These are focused on compound bows but the bulk of them also apply to recurve/longbow shooters. (available from *www.robinhoodvideos.com*)
- *Total Archery* by KiSik Lee and Robert deBondt
  One of the few unimpeachable sources on optimal recurve form. (available at *www.usarchery.org* and other online stores)
- *Archery: The Art of Repetition* by Simon S. Needham Now in paperback this book joins McKinney's, Frangilli's, and Lee/deBondt's as all in one references on Olympic-style archery. There is also a really cool companion DVD that offers one of the best O-style recurve bow setup demonstrations I have seen.

- *Bow and Arrow*, by Larry Wise
  Great book from a master coach, archer, and bow mechanic on all aspects of compound bow equipment (available from Stackpole Books, 800.READ-NOW).
- *Bringing Arrow Building Home* (presented by John Kleman)
  This video "how to" covers building and maintaining arrows (available from The Bohning Company, 616.229.4247).

- *1 Cam vs. 2 Cam Bows—Beyond Tuning*, by Larry Wise
  Master archer and coach Larry Wise compares the differences between round wheel and cam bows, one and two cam bows and even shows how to plot a draw-force curve (available from *www.robinhoodvideos.com*).
- *Easton Arrow Seminar* (presented by Ed Eliason)
  This three video set covers virtually everything you need to know about building and maintaining and tuning arrows (available from *www.robinhoodvideos.com*).
- *Mastering Bow Tuning* by James Park
  Australian James Park has written a number of books like this one which came out first on CD for easy distribution.

- *Professional String Making* (presented by Larry Wise)
  This video covers everything you need to know about building strings, cables, yokes, tied-on nock locators, D-loops, etc. (available from *www.robinhoodvideos.com*).
- *Simple Maintenance for Archery* by Ruth Rowe and Alan Henderson
  Every archery instructor needs a copy of this book! Step-by-step procedures for building arrows, tying on nocking point locators, replacing center servings, etc. (available from *www.qproductsarchery.com*).
- *Understanding Arrow Flight* (presented by Bob, Terry, and Michelle Ragsdale)
  If you prefer a video approach, this video from the Precision Shooting

Equipment (PSE) Corporation describes all of the steps in building arrows.

Understanding Release Aids
If you prefer a video approach, this video from the Precision Shooting Equipment (PSE) Corporation describes the use of various release aids.

Tuning Your Compound Bow, 4th Edition by Larry Wise
Great little book from a master coach and archer. (available from Target Communications, *www.deerinfo.com*)

Articles from Archery Focus Magazine

This may seem a little self-serving, but I hope not. *Archery Focus* magazine (yes, I am its Editor) was created by Rick McKinney and partners, who set its initial course including an OnLine version. All this was in place before I became involved. Now, here's the special part. An OnLine subscription provides six new issues (in PDF format) in the year but also access to all of the articles ever published! It is like getting all of the back-issues for free.

The OnLine Edition was designed as a archer's and coach's repository by its creators and we are continuing with that. Subscribe for a year and then you can read, download, and/or print any of hundreds of articles (around 900 at last count, not counting editorials, etc.). The whole idea is to get the information out to people who can use it. More information, including a sample copy, is available at *www.archeryfocus.com*.

As a sample of the kinds of articles available, here is a short selection--

- *Getting More Bang for Your Archery Buck* by Alan Rudolph (Vol 5, No. 3) How to make low-cost (even free) archery equipment for your programs!.
- *Video as a Training Tool* by Mark Lonsdale (Vol 6, No. 1) Everything you need to know about how to videotape archers.
- *Aiming and Sighting* by Larry Wise (Vol 5, No. 5)
- *Assessment* by Alison Rhodius (Vol 6, No. 6))
- *Becoming a Better Coach* by Lisa Franseen, Ph.D. (Vol 4, No. 4)
- *Comfort Zones* by Lisa Franseen, Ph.D. (Vol 4, No. 6)
- *Does Positive Self-talk Really Work?* by Lisa Franseen, Ph.D. (Vol 5, No. 6)
- *Don't Keep a Diary, Keep a Performance Journal* by Lanny Bassham (Vol 9, No. 1)
- *Goal Setting-Process or Outcome?* by Lanny Bassham (Vol 8, No. 1)
- *How to Level Your Compound Bow Sight* by Gene Lueck (Vol 6, No. 4) All to set all three axes on a bowsight are demonstrated.
- *Make Your Own Ethafoam™ Targets* by Ty Pelfrey (Vol 7, No. 3) Want targets you can lug around? Here's how to make them.
- *Making Your Students Mentally Tough* by Lisa Franseen, Ph.D. (Vol 4, No. 1&2)
- *Perfect Sight Tapes for Your Target Bow* by Steve Ruis (Vol 8, No. 2) Once you've printed out a beautiful computer-generated sight tape, how to put it on the bow and make it weatherproof.

- *Pressure—Is It Friend or Foe?* by Lanny Bassham (Vol 7, No. 2)
- *Rain . . . I Hate Rain!* by Karl A. Stolleis (Vol 4 No 3) All about rain gear and how to use it.
- *Shooting FITA Field Unmarked Distances* by Tim Mundon (Vol 6, No. 3) This article describes distance estimating/ranging techniques for unmarked yardage shots.
- *Shooting in the Wind and Rain* by Bernie Pellerite (Vol 4, No. 2)
- *Stop the Sun, Not the Fun!* by Pedro Serraheiro (Vol 4, No. 5) How to prevent overexposure to the sun and what to do when it happens.
- *Stringwalking the Compound Bow* by Charley Washburn (Vol 5, No. 5). This article from Archery Focus magazine is as good an introduction to stringwalking as you will find. Applies to recurves, too.
- *Target Panic!!!* by Lisa Franseen, Ph.D. (Vol 5, No. 3)
- *The 7 Habits of Successful Olympic Round Shooters* by Lloyd Brown
- *The Importance of Practice Sessions That Have a Plan* by Mike Gerard (Vol 3, No. 4)
- *The Very Last Word on Shooting Up and Down Hill* by Steve Ruis (Vol 3, No. 5) There is plenty more that could be said, but this is a good start.
- *Visualization* by Lisa Franseen, Ph.D. (Vol 1, No. 5 and Vol 2, No. 1)
- *Why Does Canting Work?* by Aaron Stone (Vol 7, No. 4)
- *Why You Need to Use a D-Loop* by George Chapman (Vol 7, No. 5) Master Coach George Chapman explains the whys of using a D-loop on your compound bow before showing you the simplest and most secure way of tying one on.

About the Author

Steve Ruis is an avid archer and coach. He has a Level 4 Coaching Certificate from USA Archery and a Master Coach certificate from the National Field Archery Association. Since 1999, he has been the editor of *Archery Focus* magazine which is distributed worldwide and is now being translated into Italian, French, German, and Spanish. He has written numerous articles about archery and coaching for that magazine and for others. He has medalled in national- and state-level competitions but his proudest archery accomplishment is being a three-time club champion of the Nevada County Sportsmens Club (Nevada City, CA). He is co-editor of *Precision Archery* (with Claudia Stevenson) which has sold over 11,000 copies since its publication in October 2003.

Notes

Notes

Notes

Notes

Notes

13597793R00073

Made in the USA
Lexington, KY
09 February 2012